D0545593

BACKPACKER'S BRITAIN
Volume 2: Wales

ABOUT THE AUTHOR

Graham's love of wild places and wildlife has taken him to all corners of the World. Today, having had 15 books published to date, he works in a number of fields in addition to being a writer. Part of his time is taken up working as an ecological surveyor, most recently for the Royal Society for the Protection of Birds, and for the British Trust for Ornithology, but he also runs navigation courses under the name of the East Anglia Navigation School in association with the National Navigation Award Scheme. He lives in the Cambridgeshire Fens, and spends his spare time enjoying photography, wildlife watching, rock climbing, cycling, and drinking real ale.

Other Cicerone guides by the author:
Backpacker's Britain Volume 1: Northern England
Backpacker's Britain Volume 3: Northern Scotland
Backpacker's Britain Volume 4: Central and Southern Scottish Highlands
Walking on the Orkney and Shetland Isles

BACKPACKER'S BRITAIN
Volume Two: Wales

by
Graham Uney

2 POLICE SQUARE, MILNTHORPE, CUMBRIA LA7 7PY
www.cicerone.co.uk

© Graham Uney 2004
Reprinted 2009 (with updates)
ISBN-13: 978 1 85284 408 0
ISBN-10: 1 85284 408 6

Printed by KHL Printing, Singapore

ACKNOWLEDGEMENTS

This book would not be possible without the support of my partner, Olivia, and without the friendship of the many people with whom I have shared a hill day in Wales. These are too numerous to mention, but Beryl and Dick Tudhope should certainly be singled out.

ADVICE TO READERS

Readers are advised that, while every effort is made by our authors to ensure the accuracy of guidebooks as they go to print, changes can occur during the lifetime of an edition. Please check the Cicerone website (www.cicerone.co.uk) for any updates before planning your trip. It is also advisable to check information on such things as transport, accommodation and shops locally. Even rights of way can be altered over time. We are always grateful for information about any discrepancies between a guidebook and the facts on the ground, sent by email to info@cicerone.co.uk or by post to Cicerone, 2 Police Square, Milnthorpe LA7 7PY.

Front cover: Heading up Crib Goch to Snowdon (Walk 3)

CONTENTS

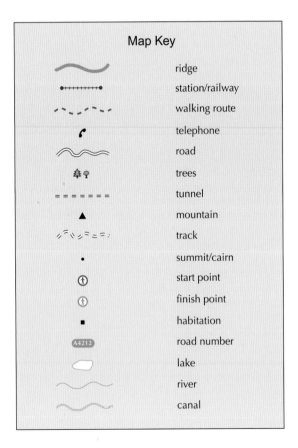

Map Key

～	ridge
•++++++++•	station/railway
⌒‿⌒‿	walking route
☎	telephone
≈≈≈	road
🌲🌳	trees
= = = = = = =	tunnel
▲	mountain
⌒‿⌒	track
•	summit/cairn
🚶	start point
🚶	finish point
■	habitation
A4212	road number
⬭	lake
～	river
～	canal

Location of Walks

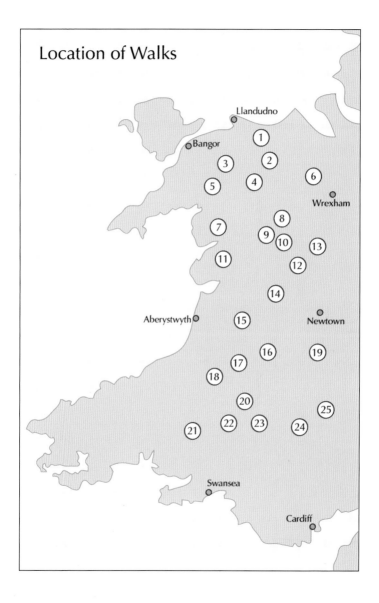

Backpacking in Mynydd du, Walk 21

INTRODUCTION

The mountains of Britain encompass surely one of the richest, most diverse landscapes to be found anywhere in the world and this great richness that we enjoy throughout the country can be seen mirrored in miniature in Wales. Only in Britain can the hill-bound walker leave his home in the city and be among hill and mountain ranges of such wonderful openness and scale within such a short space of time. Indeed most of our major cities are within an hour's drive of the nearest mountain range or national park. This closeness to our main conurbations has led to the great British 'weekend away' among the hills. Some people go in search of rock to climb, birds to watch, rivers to canoe or summits to reach, while many others are happy to pursue all of these activities, and more, to an equal degree. The wild mountains and moorland areas of Wales enjoy more than their fair share of this 'accessible inaccessibility'. The major mountain ranges of Wales are all easily reached from the main road systems of England. Snowdon, the Glyderau and Carneddau can all be easily reached from Liverpool or Manchester via the main A55 coast road, while the cwms of the southern ranges – the Brecon Beacons, Black

Descending Y Lliwedd, Walk 3

9

Walking above Crug Nywe, Walk 24

Mountains, Fforest Fawr and Mynydd Du all ring to the happy talk of folk from the Midlands, the Welsh Valleys and the south west. Perhaps the only truly inaccessible parts of Wales are those around the Elan Valley Reservoirs near Rhayader, and even these hills can give a simple days expedition if all you want to do is to reach the two main summits between breakfast and supper from your home just over the English border.

Many areas are best explored over a period of time, and so the weekend walker will often take a tent and sleeping bag with him on his forays into the wilderness. This is surely the best way of getting to know a particular part of the country. Crossing a range from end to end, or climbing a set of peaks around a desolate valley will introduce the walker to hitherto unknown regions, and where such a trip involves the commitment of an overnight stopover, so much the better. To spend a night in a primitive but comfortable way among our mountains, waking to a dewy dawn of croaking choughs on crags high above your bed, or neighing fell ponies racing around grassy slopes is one of life's great pleasures, and one that is only open to those with a will to discover these quiet places, and to make an albeit temporary home among our mountains and wild shores.

Of course, there is much to be discovered within the various mountain ranges of Britain, though indeed, some of our coastlines and lesser hill ranges deserve mention in this book too, for they are just as vital a component of our natural heritage as any of our higher but no more grand regions. There is a limitless variety of possible backpacking routes throughout the country, all as good as each other in terms of sense of achievement to be had from a successful trip, and for this reason alone this volume covers only Wales. The first book in this series covered northern England, and others to follow will detail backpacking routes in southern Scotland, northern Scotland, southern England, and Ireland respectively.

Twenty-five of the greatest backpacking routes within the boundaries of Wales are described here, all but two taking only two days to complete, with an overnight stop wild camping or spent either at a bothy, a youth hostel or a campsite. These routes should all be suitable for a weekend away among the hills, and as the other two longer walks take just three days to complete, they too should be achievable for those who enjoyed the two-day walks. Here I feel it necessary to emphasise that although this book contains what are in my opinion the very best backpacking walks in the region covered, there is endless scope for further exploration. This guide should be seen only as an introduction, an aperitif perhaps, for other longer routes that can be planned and tackled by those

Moel Meirch, Walk 4

who have gained experience through following the routes described here.

This book is laid out along simple lines. Each chapter covers one route, and begins with a fact file and walk summary. These give details of where to start the walk, the number of days needed to complete it, the distance of each day's walk, and where to stay overnight. This latter note will help you decide whether to carry equipment for camping, youth hostelling, bothying, or staying in a bunk barn. The Ordnance Survey maps needed along the way, and a brief area summary are given at the beginning of each walk description.

The sketch maps are intended to be used only as such – it is strongly advised that the relevant OS map is used during the walk, and that steps are taken beforehand to learn the complexities of navigation. Many useful books have been published which can help with this, and navigation courses are regularly organised by the author (see Appendix 2 for the address). Descriptive text is given in green type to distinguish it from the route directions, and place names from the sketch maps are highlighted in bold type to aid orientation.

SAFETY IN THE HILLS

Great tomes have been written on this subject, and readers should refer to the specialist books suggested in the bibliography. Suffice it to say that, for the most part, common sense is all

that is required. By this I mean simply going into the hills well equipped for the task in hand, both in taking the right gear with you and in having the necessary navigation skills to accurately find your way in all weathers. Many people stress the importance of leaving written word with a responsible party before heading off into the hills, and indeed this is good advice for those new to hillwalking. However, for me, one of the real joys of hillwalking, and backpacking in particular, is the freedom that it provides, including the liberty to change plans if, for instance, you have found the going easier than expected or the weather has improved and you find yourself wanting to extend your stay in the mountains. This is not possible, and certainly should not ever be considered, if written word of your intentions has been left. The choice is up to the individual, and generally the best advice is to leave a route card, although if you do this you must stick to it rigidly. Obviously, if you choose not to leave a route card you will be very much on your own should an accident occur.

NAVIGATION

This is the one subject that gets people most flummoxed, or at least it is something that many hillgoers claim to have mastered, but would no doubt struggle with should push come to shove. It is beyond the scope of this book to go into any great detail on this fascinating art, and it is hoped that anyone heading off into the hills would first book themselves onto a navigation course organised by professionals. Having said that, a few very general pointers are given here.

The main skill to master is that of setting the map. To oversimplify things, it is perhaps best to point out that the top of all OS maps is Grid North, and the red directional needle (the one that turns in the compass housing) points to Magnetic North. It is an easy matter to place the compass onto the map and turn the map around until this needle is pointing to the top of the map. This will then set the map in line with all of the features on the ground – walls, fences, streams, hills – everything on the map should be in line with their corresponding ground features. This is actually slightly flawed, as Grid North and Magnetic North are

not exactly the same. Basically, the compass points slightly left of Grid North at the moment, and the key at the edge of the map will tell you how many degrees the difference is for any year. You then just add that difference to the dial on your compass and you are in business.

To measure distances on the map you need to know the scale – usually either 1:50,000 (OS Landranger maps) or 1:25,000 (OS Explorer, Outdoor Leisure and Pathfinder maps, and Harvey's Superwalker maps). You can use the scale on the bottom of the map to find out how many millimetres on your compass represent 100 metres on the ground, and using this information you should be able to measure any distance on the map with some sort of accuracy. So far so good, but then you need to know how many double steps you take to walk 100 metres. This

Aran Benllyn, Walk 9

obviously varies according to the size of your legs, so it is something you will have to work out for yourself. Most people take between 55 and 80 double steps to walk 100 metres, but bear in mind that this is on the flat, on a good surface. Your pacing will differ if you head uphill or downhill, and will also be different over rough terrain such as deep heather or soft snow. You can practise all of this by either going out with someone who already knows how many paces they take to 100 metres, or by going on a navigation course.

Another way of measuring distances, and the preferred method over longer distances (you don't want to spend all day counting paces!) is timing. The average walking speed is 5km per hour (kmh), so at this speed it will take 12 minutes to walk 1000 metres (1km) on flat ground. Most people add 1 minute to the overall time of a set leg of the journey for every 10-metre contour climbed during that leg. However, for timing to be really useful you do need to know your own walking speed. I personally prefer to walk at 6km/h, whereas others walk at 4km/h or even slower. The other problem with timing is that it will be different according to how heavy your rucksack is, or how tired you are, or the type of terrain you are walking over. It is best to experiment with timing over known distances to get the hang of it.

15

The only true way to learn navigation is out on the hill, initially by going on a course, then by regularly practising the techniques on your own.

EQUIPMENT

This is a very subjective issue. A browse through any outdoor retailer's shop will reveal a bewildering array of boots, jackets, tents, sleeping bags, stoves, maps, compasses, and those little pouches for keeping your mobile phone safe and sound. In short, there is no shortage of gear and gizmos you can buy for the hills. Some of it is essential, other bits and pieces less so.

To get started in backpacking, you will probably find that you already possess some of the essential items – most aspiring backpackers have been active in the outdoors previously and will usually own a pair of boots, a waterproof jacket and overtrousers set, and probably a compass, map case, torch and first aid kit.

To head out for a night in the hills you will need to add a good sleeping bag to this list. There are basically two types of bag – down filled and synthetic. Down is lighter in weight but useless if you get it wet, whereas the synthetic is heavier but retains some of its warming properties when wet. Synthetic is usually a good deal cheaper than the better quality down-filled bag.

A good mat under your sleeping bag is essential to keep you insulated from the cold ground beneath.

Foam mats are cheap, but better is a Thermarest-type which is air-filled. These are far more comfortable, but much more expensive.

Then you'll need a tent to put over yourself. I have used a number of different makes and models over the years, but for most people the best advice is to get the lightest tent you can for the seasons you intend to use it in, and to pay the most you can afford. Hopefully you can automatically scrub all the next to useless models of tent from your shopping list. I have recently been asked to use a Hilleberg Akto, which really is superb for all-season camping, even in the wildest of areas. It is the lightest tent I have ever backpacked with, is easy to pitch, and gives me the confidence to go anywhere at any time of year.

Next you'll need a stove of some sort. Gas is a popular fuel favourite, while meths-burning Trangia's are very often seen being used by youth groups. The Trangia is a very safe stove and has the benefit of having no working parts to break. It is light and easy to use, although it does take a lot longer to boil water for cooking than almost any other camping stove I have used. Personally I would always go for a Coleman Duel Fuel model. They are very efficient, and you will be supping your soup with one of these beauties before most of your mates have even raised a bubble in their pots with other stove models.

On top of your camping equipment it is also a good idea to have spare, warm, dry clothing in your rucksack if you are out for anything more than a single day in the hills.

Obviously, you'll need a larger rucksack than your daysack to carry all of this extra kit up and down the hills, and again, there are countless makes and models on the market. Go to an outdoor shop and try them all on, aiming for something around 60–70 litres in size. Get the assistant in the shop to fill the rucksacks with tents and other heavy gear, then carry each one around the shop to see which feels the best for you.

Once you have set off on your walk, aim to have everything in your rucksack, rather than have things hanging on the outside. Apart from looking better, this also helps to distribute the weight more evenly and will make for a more enjoyable backpacking trip.

FOOD

Food should be nutritious and palatable, and you should plan to carry enough to fulfil your energy needs for the duration of the trip, plus have some high-energy foods spare in case of emergency. Generally speaking most people burn between 3000 to 4000 calories a day when they are backpacking, and it is recommended that you should replace this throughout the day – a backpacking trip is not the time to go on a diet! Try to balance your daily intake so that you have around 60–65% carbohydrates,

25–30% fats and 10–15% protein. Plenty of fluids are essential, partly to replace that lost through sweating, and partly to help you digest food more efficiently. Try to spread your daily food intake out over the day, eating little and often throughout the walk, rather than stopping for a huge food-fest at lunchtime and spending the rest of the day snoozing it off!

It is hard to try to eat similar foods to those you would normally eat at home when on a backpacking trip. The best advice is to experiment over different trips, and this can indeed become a great part of the whole backpacking experience.

As for spare emergency food, most people throw a few chocolate bars, flapjacks or high-energy bars into the bottom of their rucksacks. I know many people who always eat their 'emergency rations' long before the trip is over, and of course that is not ideal. Some people deliberately take with them something that they don't actually like, which is a good idea, so long as it is high in energy, whereas I have heard it recommended that you wrap your emergency rations in sticky tape, making it very difficult to get into. This is fine until that emergency occurs, and you still can't get into it!

ACCESS AND THE BACKPACKER

It should be noted that while the author has enjoyed many days backpacking along these routes, and has never encountered hostility from landowners,

Crossing a limestone pavement on Walk 21

many of the walks described, or at least some sections of most of them, lie off the public rights of way system. A sensible approach is usually all that is required – keeping within the bounds of the Country Code, leaving nothing but footprints and taking nothing but photographs and memories. Camping wild does not imply that the land is not owned, and it is suggested that you seek the landowner's permission before doing so. Neither the author nor the publisher can accept responsibility for the actions of readers of this book with regard to access to private land. The inclusion of a route in this book does not imply that the reader has a right to walk there or to camp along the route.

A NOTE ON MEASURING DISTANCES AND HEIGHTS

Although many hillwalkers today still like to deal in feet, yards and miles, with modern Ordnance Survey maps this seems a little like making a lot of hard work for yourself. Maps today give all heights in metres above sea level, while grid squares are a kilometre across, and I feel that it is ridiculous to continue using an archaic system that does not bear any relation to that used by our cartographers. After all, maps are the single most important tools for the hillwalker, and so this guide gives all measurements in the metric form. Those walkers wishing to deal in the imperial will no doubt be well used to converting the two systems, and will therefore take great delight in doing so with all measurements quoted within this book.

1 – The High Carneddau

Total Distance:	42km
Daily Distances:	1) 21km 2) 21km
Maps:	OS Outdoor Leisure, sheet 17 *Snowdon and Conwy Valley*
Starting Point:	The Aber Falls car park by the bridge at grid ref. SH 662 720. This is reached through the village of Abergwyngregyn off the main A55 coast road.

Area Summary: The Carneddau makes up one of the largest upland areas in Wales, comprising a vast land of rough moorland cut into deep cwms or valleys on all sides and rising to a central ridge that itself breaks into seven summits over 915m. It is bordered to the north by the coast at Conwy Bay, to the east by the estuary of the Afon Conwy, to the south by the deep trough of the Ogwen Valley and to the west by the trench of the Nant Ffrancon valley. For me, the Carneddau is one of the best ranges in Wales for backpacking routes, offering endless scope and good views all around, coupled with a slightly quieter and away-from-it-all feel to it that is not possible in the nearby Glyderau to the south across the Ogwen Valley.

Walk Summary: A tough walk over fairly easy terrain, starting at the Aber Falls near Abergwyngregyn village on the north coast. The walk starts on the quiet hills of Drum and Foel-fras on the main ridge before descending to the beautiful valley of the Afon Dulyn to the south-east. It then takes the backpacker around the lower slopes of a ridge and into the valley holding the Llyn Eigiau Reservoir before tackling the slopes of Pen Llithrig y Wrach and Pen yr Helgi Du. The route then takes you

Transport:	Buses run between the coastal towns and cities along the A55. Check that the driver will set you down at Abergwyngregyn.
Accommodation and Supplies:	Loads of B&Bs in Bangor just up the A55, or try the youthhostel there (tel. 01248 353516). There are also plenty of shops and a couple of supermarkets in Bangor. There are no shops along the route.
Overnight Options:	There are two campsites in the Ogwen Valley: Gwern Gof Uchaf (grid ref. SH 673 605) and Gwern Gof Isaf (grid ref. SH 685 602), the latter of which also has a bunkhouse (tel. 01690 720276 to book). Also try Idwal Cottage Youth Hostel (grid ref. SH 648 604) at the western end of Llyn Ogwen (tel. 01248 600225). They will even let members camp outside and use their facilities if they are busy. Going on to Idwal Cottage adds an extra 5km to the overall distance.

down into the Ogwen Valley for the night. The second day starts with a steep climb up Pen yr Ole Wen at the southern end of the main ridge before heading along the ridge itself as far as Garnedd Uchaf where it heads north into remote country around Drosgl. It is generally easy going with some boggy ground; there are paths on some sections of the route, but others need careful navigation to follow safely.

Day One: Cwm Eigiau and the Slippery Hill of the Witch

From the car park start by crossing the bridge, heading eastwards along the tarmac lane as it climbs steeply up to emerge from the trees beneath the high slopes of the north Carneddau. The road becomes a track and continues eastwards to meet another track at a crossroads on the northern ridge of a little hill known as Foel Ganol at 393m. ◄

At the crossroads turn right and climb gently uphill around the nose of the ridge to a little col below the

This track follows the course of a Roman Road.

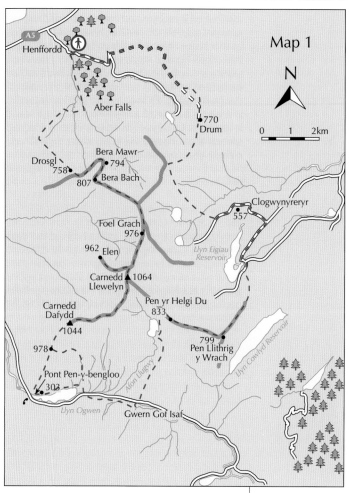

Map 1

N

| 0 | 1 | 2km |

Henffordd

A5

Aber Falls

•770 Drum

Bera Mawr
•794
Bera Bach
807

Drosgl
758•

Clogwynyreryr
•557

Foel Grach
976•

962 •Elen

Llyn Eigiau
Reservoir

Carnedd ▲1064
Llewelyn

Pen yr Helgi Du
833•

Carnedd
Dafydd
▲1044

978•

799•
Pen Llithrig
y Wrach

Llyn Cowlyd Reservoir

Pont Pen-y-bengloo
303•

Afon Llugwy

Llyn Ogwen

Gwern Gof Isaf

pudding-shape of Drum's north ridge. Continuing along the track will lead to the ancient cairn at the summit of **Drum** at 770m. You are now on the main ridge of the Carneddau and should set off from the summit in a

21

south-westerly direction down to a grassy col. The route climbs steeply up to the first big hill of the walk, Foel-fras at 942m. The summit is marked by a trig point and lies to the north of the large dry-stone wall.

From Foel-fras a stile leads over the wall and you should head downhill to the southeast towards the out-flow of the Dulyn Reservoir which comes into view as you lose height. Cross the stream at the outflow and head diagonally uphill to the east to pick up a track at **Clogwynyreryr**. Follow the track around the ridge and down to a sheepfold, then head southeast out along the track to the end of a minor road at Trasbwll. Here turn right and follow a track to the dam at the outflow of the Llyn Eigiau Reservoir. Cross the dam and bear right, looking for a split in the public right of way at a building. Take the path heading initially south, uphill to Hafod-y-Rhiw, climbing steeply beyond that building to a point on the north ridge of Pen Llithrig y Wrach where the path crosses over and starts off down the other side. Here turn right and follow the ridge southwest up to the exposed summit of **Pen Llithrig y Wrach** at 799m. The summit is right at the edge of the drop into the Cowlyd Reservoir to the east. ◂

A vague path leads westwards from the summit across open slopes before leading you down to the little col known as Bwlch y Tri Marchog. Here head west, starting around the southern side of a prominent knoll, then picking up a good path up the long east ridge of **Pen yr Helgi Du**. A cairn is reached on the bald summit slopes, but the true top lies a little further on at 833m. ◂

From the summit you can head south down the long ridge known as Y Braich into Ogwen, but those with a head for heights might like to tackle the delightful little scramble down to Bwlch Eryl Farchog. It is very easy but quite exposed, although it hardly adds any distance on to the overall tally for the day.

For this short alternative, leave the summit of Pen yr Helgi Du by heading north-west on a narrowing ridge, then scramble easily down to the col at Bwlch Eryl Farchog. The route down is obvious, and a path

The name Pen Llithrig y Wrach means 'Slippery Hill of the Witch', although its derivation has been lost in time.

Pen yr Helgi Du's name is another whose deriva-tion has been lost over the years. It means 'Head of the Black Hound'.

The summit of
Foel-fras

leads the way. From the bwlch (which is just the Welsh word for a col) a path leads off the ridge to the south and descends in steep zigzags down to the eastern shore of Ffynnon Llugwy Reservoir. Follow the vague path on the eastern side of the reservoir, picking up the tarmac access road at 550m. Follow this road downhill to join the A5 at a junction by a gate down in the Ogwen Valley. Turn left for 200m along the A5. This is where those coming down Y Braich from the summit of Pen yr Helgi Du will re-join the main route. A footpath leads south to cross the Afon Llugwy ('afon' meaning 'river'), and then picks up an ancient route at a T-junction. Turn right along this well-marked track and follow it up into Ogwen passing Gwern Gof Isaf then Gwern Gof Uchaf campsites. Those heading for Idwal Cottage must continue along the track to rejoin the A5 beneath the towering ridge of Tryfan, from where you should cross the road and follow the path to Tal-y-Llyn Ogwen farm. Here a public footpath leads around the back of Llyn Ogwen ('llyn' meaning 'lake') to bring you out at Idwal Cottage.

Day Two: The High Carneddau

Start the day by climbing the daunting-looking mountain to the north of Llyn Ogwen. This is Pen yr Ole Wen, and depending on where you stayed the night there are two options for climbing it:

1) From either of the two campsites follow the track out to its end at the A5 and take the footpath to Tal y Llyn Ogwen farm. From here signs point the way up the steep slope to the right of the stream issuing from the hanging valley, or cwm, above. The path soon crosses the stream, the Afon Lloer and brings you out into the cwm near the beautiful tarn of Ffynnon Lloer. Just before the tarn is reached the path heads off up the ridge to the west, making directly for the summit of Pen yr Ole Wen at 978m.

2) From Idwal Cottage cross the main road and head left to cross the road bridge that spans the Rhaeadr Ogwen, the famous Ogwen Falls. A gap in the wall on the right gives access to a path that leads up the improbable-looking slopes above. The path is lost at times, but a determined effort soon has all the steep slopes behind and the summit underfoot. There is no scrambling along this route of ascent, although first impressions may lead you to think otherwise. ◄

Both routes meet on the summit, from where you should start off north-westwards initially, following the obvious ridge around the head of Cwm Lloer to the next main summit, **Carnedd Dafydd**. The summit cairn lies a little way off the main path, so summit-baggers will wish to deviate here – only by a few metres though. The summit lies at 1044m above sea level.

Pen yr Ole Wen means 'Hill of the White Light', another obscurity. Its summit is a fantastic viewpoint from which to look southwards over the Glyderau and the hollow of Cwm Idwal with its famous slabs and notch of the Devil's Kitchen.

Carnedd Dafydd and its higher twin to the north, Carnedd Llewelyn, are said to be named after Llewelyn the Great and his successor, although others claim that they are named after the last of the Welsh Princes, Llywelyn ap Gruffdd and his brother. We shall never really know, but to be honest it hardly seems to matter.

From Carnedd Dafydd the ridge bends around to the east. Follow this for 1½km to the top of the ridge known as Craig Llugwy where in mist the route seems to continue eastwards. This is not the way however. You should head northwards onto the narrow ridge then up to the broad slopes of **Carnedd Llewelyn**. A large cairn and summit shelter mark the top at 1064m. This is the highest peak of the Carneddau range.

Another big peak lies over to the north-west from Carnedd Llewelyn, although being off the main ridge only the summit-bagger need bother. That said, it does provide excellent views back onto the ridge and is well worth it. From Carnedd Llewelyn head northwest down stony ground to a narrow col, then follow the ridge around to the right to reach the summit of **Yr Elen**, a fine peak at 962m. Retrace your steps back to Carnedd Llewelyn, and then head north on the main path to **Foel Grach's** summit at 976m.

Buzzards are common in the Carneddau

North from here the Carneddau opens out into broad slopes with jagged teeth of rock jutting out of the moorland grasses. A number of summits dot this expanse, and the route takes in the main peaks of this northern part of the range.

Head north from Foel Grach, noting a little emergency shelter tucked in under the northern slopes of the summit. The route drops down to a broad, grassy col, then climbs up to Garnedd Uchaf at 926m. Here you will find a fine rock-splintered summit. Leave the summit by heading north-west to the rock pinnacles of Yr Aryg, reached easily over short grass, then north-west again for the tor-like summit of **Bera Bach** at 807m.

Scrambling on
Bera Mawr

Bera Bach and Bera
Mawr are actually
misnamed. In Welsh
'bach' means 'small'
while 'mawr' means
'big'. The old survey-
ors clearly got the
measurements wrong
when they put these
names down on the
early maps.

Eight hundred metres northeast of Bera Bach stands its smaller neighbour, **Bera Mawr**, at 794m. It is an easy, though occasionally boggy, crossing to the fine summit pinnacles here. A short scramble leads to the top of the highest point. ◄

Leaving Bera Mawr you need to contour westwards around the northern slopes of Bera Bach at about 720m. This will lead you over rough grass and some boggy ground to a col below the little dome of **Drosgl**. The grass gives way to scree and stone as you climb this last summit to the huge cairn at 758m. Head north-west from the summit down to a broad grassy col near the weird little hill known as Gyrn, then pick up a path downhill on the north side of the Afon Gam. This takes you easily to a track far down the slopes that should be taken to the right. It leads beneath the Aber Falls, then out along the true right bank of the Afon Rhaeadr Fawr back to the bridge at the car park.

2 – The Glyderau and Southern Carneddau from Capel Curig

Total Distance:	43km
Daily Distances:	1) 24km 2) 19km
Maps:	OS Outdoor Leisure, sheet 17 *Snowdon and Conwy Valley*
Starting Point:	Park in Capel Curig in the National Park Car Park, behind the Pinnacles Café and Joe Browns' (grid ref. SH 720 583)

Area Summary: The Glyders, or Glyderau as they should more correctly be known, are not surprisingly one of the best known and best loved mountain ranges in Britain. They comprise some of the most spectacular individual summits south of the Scottish Border, each linked by jagged ridges and slabby faces of good clean rock, and with mountains of such individual character as Tryfan, Glyder Fach and Glyder Fawr as the focal point of the range their popularity will always be assured. There are other aspects to this range though, including the quiet, grassy ridge over the two summits of Gallt yr Ogof and Y Foel Goch by which this route gains the main heights, and the equally breathtaking but slightly less rugged mountains of the Elidir group to the north of the Glyderau, separated from them by the low col at the head of the Devil's Kitchen. In complete contrast the mountains of the southern Carneddau across the trench of the Ogwen valley form long whale-back ridges falling in what are largely grassy slopes to deep-cut cwms. This part of the Carneddau throws out a subsidiary ridge to the east down to the Llyn Cowlyd Reservoir, and beyond here the terrain changes to heathery moorland crowned by little rocky peaks.

Walk Summary: A long, hard walk over some of the toughest mountains in Wales. Day One starts easily enough along the Gallt yr Ogof ridge to Y Foel Goch, but then takes the backpacker down to the low col below the south ridge of Tryfan. A short though rocky scramble leads to the top of this giant of a mountain. Back at the col the route heads up scree to the summit of Glyder Fach before crossing the open wasteland around Castell y Gwynt, the 'Castle of the Winds' to the high point of the trip, Glyder Fawr. A big descent leads to Llyn y Cŵm, from where it is possible to cut out the Elidirs altogether if need be, although the main route tackles Y Garn direct up its southern face. Pleasant ridge walking then follows around the circuit of four summits of the Elidirs, finishing on Carnedd y Filiast. A way is then taken down steep slopes to the old road up the Nant Ffrancon Valley to Idwal Cottage Youth Hostel. Day Two starts steeply up the direct route to the summit of Pen yr Ole Wen in the Carneddau. The main Carneddau ridge is then followed around to Carnedd Llewelyn before heading southeast to Pen yr Helgi Du and Pen Llithrig y Wrach. The route descends to the head of the Llyn Cowlyd Reservoir before tackling the boggy and long slopes of Creigiau Gleision. Before heading back to Capel Curig you must head northwards to take in the northern summit of this fine little hill, returning to Capel Curig via the delightful wooded valley of the Crafnant.

Transport: Buses run up the valley to Capel Curig from Betws-y-Coed which in turn is served by buses and trains from Llandudno.

Accommodation and supplies: There are loads of B&Bs in Betws-y-Coed, including a bunkhouse at the Glan Aber Hotel, or try the youth hostel in Capel Curig (tel. 01690 720225). You will also find plenty of shops and a small supermarket there. There are no shops along the route, although you can buy a few self-catering supplies at Idwal Cottage Youth Hostel.

Overnight Options: Use the youth hostel at Idwal Cottage, or ask to camp there is you want a room to yourself! (tel. 01248 600225)

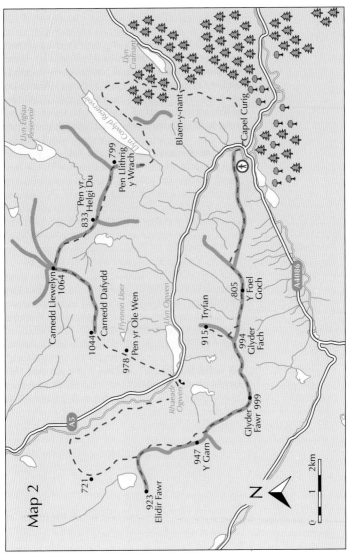

Map 2

N

Llyn Crafnant

Llyn Cowlyd Reservoir

Blaen-y-nant

Capel Curig

Llyn Eigiau Reservoir

799 Pen Llithrig y Wrach

Pen yr Helgi Du 833

Carnedd Llewelyn 1064

1044

Carnedd Dafydd

978 Pen yr Ole Wen

Ffynnon Lloer

Llyn Ogwen

Tryfan 915

805 Y Foel Goch

994 Glyder Fach

A5

Rhaeadr Ogwen

721

923 Elidir Fawr

947 Y Garn

Glyder Fawr 999

A4086

0   1   2km

Day One: Across the Glyders and Elidirs

Begin by leaving the car park from its north-west corner on the good track that heads north. This leads to the small farm at Gelli and you should look for a vague path behind the farm climbing up to the west just below a low knoll. This path soon becomes more defined as it gains height, leading first to the little hill known as Cefn y Capel, then onwards to the west as you drop to a boggy col at Bwlch Goleuni. From here the ground gets steeper, and the path leads up to the main ridge between Gallt yr Ogof and Y Foel Goch, the first two summits on this marathon ridge walk. Gallt yr Ogof's summit, at 763m, lies just off the path to the right.

Tryfan

From the summit drop down to the south-west to regain the path, then continue in the same direction to a small col with a tiny pond. The path continues up the grassy slopes above to the summit plateau of **Y Foel Goch**. There are a number of little rocky knolls on this small plateau, but the actual summit is the one on the right as you approach at 805m high.

The path now heads off westwards across very boggy ground dotted with little tarns and pools on its way to a junction of paths where the Miner's Track crosses over the ridge from Pen-y-Gwryd to the south to the Ogwen Valley in the north.

When crossing the boggy ground towards the path junction keep an eye out for the mountain goats which often gather here. Some of them sport impressive sets of horns. It is a tradition that the farmers always encouraged wild goats in the area so that they would climb onto the rocky ledges of the crags and into the gullies of the high mountains to eat the lush vegetation. The thinking behind it was that if the goats ate all the herbage the sheep would not be tempted onto this dangerous ground where they would be less at home than the goats. It is also worth looking in the pools themselves for bog bean and bottle sedges, which grow there, and you will invariably see plenty of common frogs and toads.

The huge, awe-inspiring bulk of Tryfan can be seen across the cwm to the north from the path junction, and there is a choice of routes from here, depending on whether you are tempted to tackle Tryfan's South Ridge.

Tryfan lies off the main spine of the Glyders, and to reach it you must descend to a col at 730m before facing the climb to the summit at 915m. You must then retrace your steps to the col and head back onto the main ridge to continue. Some may feel that with a heavy pack on your back this extra effort is not really worth it. If this is the case, simply continue west from the path junction to the summit of Glyder Fach where those heading for Tryfan will rejoin the main route.

To climb Tryfan start by taking the Miner's Track off to the right. This drops through a short rocky gully and leads over boulders and scree to just below the col known as Bwlch Tryfan. The path then climbs up to the high stone wall on the col itself. Those with a head for heights and some scrambling experience may wish to tackle the South Ridge Direct, although with a heavy rucksack on your back most will probably be satisfied with the easiest route. This starts over the wall and bypasses the lower rocky buttresses to the left. There are countless possible ways up this South Ridge and all lead in varying degrees of difficulty to the two large boulders, Adam and Eve, that form the highest point of the mountain.

It is said that those who can jump from Adam to Eve will become Freemen of Tryfan. It really is more a case of those with long legs will become Freemen of Tryfan as it is just a short stride for those so endowed. Others, however, are faced with a real leap of faith, as both blocks have small, sloping tops and there is a huge drop to the east down which you would not want to fall. For many it is enough just to sit below the blocks and eat their sandwiches, which is all you should feel obliged to do.

Return to Bwlch Tryfan and cross over the wall to its eastern side. From here a path can be seen climbing up the scree slope ahead, and you should follow this up onto the plateau of **Glyder Fach**. This is a mass of tors, boulders, and fallen blocks and can be confusing in mist. The summit at 994m high is itself very obvious though and lies to the south-west of the top of the scree slope

Walkers resting below Adam and Eve

which you have just climbed. It is composed of a pile of very big boulders and requires care when ascending and descending. ▸

From the summit carefully climb down off the blocks to regain the plateau. Head off to the south west, passing the spiky tor known as Castell y Gwynt (Castle of the Winds) on your right. A path is picked up here which bends around under the Castell and down to a little col at 919m, known as Bwlch y Ddwy Glyder, and from here a more obvious path heads across a stony slope westwards towards Glyder Fawr. The way is much more obvious now, although you should not make the mistake of following the cairns here – there are literally dozens of them, all seemingly leading off in different directions. Just head southwest to the spot height at 957m, then west to the main summit of **Glyder Fawr** at 999m. This is a cluster of spikes piercing the plateau and lies just off the main path.

From Glyder Fawr the path starts by heading to the west, and then turns to the north-west down stony slopes to the eastern end of Llyn y Cŵm, a lovely mountain tarn on a high pass.

Those who have had enough for the day can turn off to the right down the well-made path into the Devil's Kitchen and along the eastern shore of Llyn Idwal to Ogwen and the Idwal Cottage Youth Hostel. But for those wanting more, the route takes in a further four summits before the day is done.

Head around to the northernmost point of Llyn y Cŵm, from where you will find a broad track ascending the southern flank of Y Garn. This is a huge mountain, but the way up from here is relatively straightforward and you will soon find yourself skirting the edge of the cliffs to the right that fall into Cwm Clyd. Follow this line of cliffs to the summit of **Y Garn** at 947m.

Walk north from the summit along the obvious track, turning to the north-west and continuing along the hand-rail provided by the top edge of the cliffs on your right. This leads down to a col, then up and over the little summit of Foel-goch at 831m.

To get to the summit you pass the famous Cantilever Stone which is a huge slab of rock perched on a narrow fulcrum. You can walk out to the end and feel the vibrations from your own footsteps.

Again follow the cliff top around to the north-west, down to another col then up to the broader summit of Mynydd Perfedd, whose top lies a little way back from the edge and is marked by a large cairn.

Those wishing to extend the walk even further may want to head west from the col between Foel-goch and Mynydd Perfedd to take in the much higher summit of **Elidir Fawr**, which at 924m is the main summit of the Elidir group. Once you have reached its summit atop a long, rocky ridge you must return to Mynydd Perfedd to continue the walk. Head back east to a very narrow col, then climb up the rock ridge to the east which brings you out onto the convex dome of Mynydd Perfedd.

Take a bearing north from Mynydd Perfedd's summit to the top of Carnedd y Filiast, the last summit of the day. Stony ground leads down to the broad col between the two, then easily up to the summit cairn at 821m. ◄

The name Carnedd y Filiast translates literally into English as 'Cairn of the Greyhound Bitch', but as with so many of these old Welsh names, we do not know why it is known as such.

From the summit cairn of Carnedd y Filiast head roughly east to the edge of the cliffs that you have followed all the way from Y Garn. Turn left here and walk northwards around the rim, descending to the north-east as the cliffs move in that direction. Follow this widening ridge downhill for 600m to the old road in the Nant Ffrancon Valley at Tai-newyddion.

Turn right along this road, which is little used other than for access to the farms along its length, and follow it for 4km southwards to Idwal Cottage Youth Hostel in the Ogwen Valley.

Day Two: The Southern Carneddau and the Crafnant Valley

The day begins with a real slog. Leave the youth hostel and turn right out of the doorway and down to the main road. Turn left at the junction and walk over the bridge carrying the Afon Ogwen down the Ogwen Falls, Rhaeadr Ogwen. On the opposite side of the road by the side of the bridge a path leads straight up the steep south-western flank of **Pen yr Ole Wen**. Although daunting to look at, there can be few more direct routes up

The Elidirs

any mountain in Britain, and after a bit of weaving about around rock outcrops and up scree gullies, you soon emerge victorious on the summit at 978m.

Drop down to the col to the north-west, and follow the ridge around to the summit of **Carnedd Dafydd** at 1044m. The summit cairn lies just off the path on the right. Here the path swings to the east above the cliffs known as the Black Ladders (Ysgolion Duon) and you should follow the rim of the cliffs around, taking care where the ridge turns north-east above Craig Llugwy. Here the ridge seems to continue to the south-east, but just a few metres further on it becomes much more obvious as it makes its way north-eastwards towards the highest mountain in the Carneddau group, **Carnedd Llewelyn** at 1064m. ◄

The main ridge of the Carneddau, as followed in Chapter One, continues northwards, but at Carnedd Llewelyn's summit cairn our route heads off initially in a south-eastern direction, curving around to the east above the high cwm holding the lovely little tarn of Ffynnon Llyffnant. Follow the ridge around over rocky steps, swinging back to the south-east and down to the narrow col at Bwlch Eryl Farchog.

Continuing south-eastwards from the col, a slender ridge presents itself, and although very narrow in places, the path leads the way and is easy to follow without needing to recourse to scrambling. The ridge soon leads to the grassy summit of **Pen yr Helgi Du** at 833m.

Walk south-eastwards, swinging again to the east down the easy ridge of Pen yr Helgi Du to the Bwlch y Tri Marchog beside a little rocky knoll. A stile leads over a fence here and the short west ridge of **Pen Llithrig y Wrach** is easy, leading to the broad summit plateau with the summit cairn itself perched on the lip of the drop into the trench holding the Llyn Cowlyd Reservoir to the east.

Turning south from the summit a vague path leads down the south ridge to a bridge over the inlet for the Reservoir. Cross this, and then begin the climb up the boggy slopes of Creigiau Gleision, marked on the OS Outdoor Leisure maps at Llethr Gwyn.

Carnedd Llewelyn and Carnedd Dafydd are said to be named after Llewelyn the Great and his successor, although others claim that they are named after the last of the Welsh Princes, Llywelyn ap Gruffdd and his brother.

Creigiau Gleision is a wonderful switchback ridge of rocky tors and knolls bisected by heathery cols which are sometimes boggy. The main summit is at the spot height 678m and you will soon reach this point. Here a path will be seen leading off to the north-east. This leads to the next little summit at 634m, and you should follow this, continuing on from the summit to a fence. Turn right and follow the fence downhill, crossing to the other side for easier going. Soon you will be able to cut across to the south to the top corner of a forestry plantation. From this point a footpath takes you deep into the forest to the south, emerging on a track after a short while. The going is boggy, but if you stay on the path it soon eases. Once on the main track look for a continuation straight ahead which crosses a cleared area of forest. This path then descends to the valley bottom and you should bear right at the next track you come to which swings around to just above the private houses at Hendre.

Walk out along their access road to where the road turns sharply to the left at Blaen-y-nant. Here a green lane heads up behind the cottage and can be followed easily over a boggy col and down to the youth hostel in Capel Curig, coming out in the village just above the Snowdonia Café. Once on the road turn right and walk back to the car park behind the Pinnacle Café.

A mountain goat spied on this route

3 – The Snowdon Massif

Total Distance:	32km
Daily Distances:	1) 18km 2) 14km
Maps:	OS Outdoor Leisure, sheet 17 *Snowdon and Conwy Valley*
Starting Point:	The youth hostel in the popular mining village of Llanberis (grid ref. SH 574 597)

Area Summary: The Snowdon range is without doubt one of the grandest mountain areas in the whole of Britain. It comprises the highest mountain in the country south of Ben Lomond in the Scottish Southern Highlands, as well as some of the finest ridge walks and scrambles in Wales. The range is bordered to the east by the valley of Llanberis, to the west by that of the Nant Colwyn, to the south by the Nant Gwynant and to the north it fizzles out towards the coast on the Menai Strait. The range is made up of a number of important mountains over 2000 feet high, and this walk takes you over all of them.

Walk Summary: This is a short though tough walk over difficult terrain. Starting at the hostel in Llanberis the route begins gently enough with the mountains at the northern end of the Snowdon range around Moel Eilio, before descending to a low col at the foot of the Snowdon Ranger Track up Snowdon itself. From the summit of Snowdon a way is found over to the fine rocky ridge of Y Lliwedd, from where you descend to Pen y Pass Youth Hostel for the night. Day Two starts with a ridge scramble over the finest knife-edged crest south of the Scottish Highlands. Crib Goch is not too difficult for those with a head for heights, but **BE WARNED**, it is not a place for incompetent scramblers or those who prefer

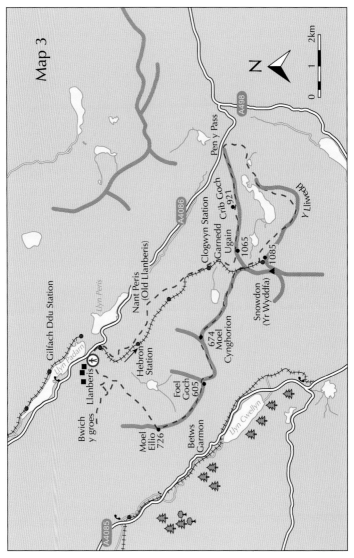

Map 3

N

0 1 2km

A498

Pen y Pass

Crib Goch
921

Y Lliwedd

A4086

Clogwyn Station

Garnedd
Ugain
1065

1085

Nant Peris
(Old Llanberis)

Snowdon
(Yr Wyddfa)

674
Moel
Cynghorion

Gilfach Ddu Station

Llyn Peris

Hebron
Station

Foel
Goch
605

Bwlch
y groes

Llanberis

Llyn Padarn

Moel
Eilio
726

Betws
Garmon

Llyn Cwellyn

A4085

Transport:	Buses run between the coastal towns and cities along the A55 to Llanberis and continue in summer up to the youth hostel at Pen y Pass where you will be spending the night.
Accommodation and supplies:	Loads of B&Bs in Llanberis, but you should try the youth hostel if you intend to park there (tel. 01286 870280). There are also plenty of shops and a couple of supermarkets in Llanberis, and you can eat well at Pete's Eats on the High Street. There is the sky-high café on the summit of Snowdon, with prices to match, but no other shops along the way.
Overnight Options:	Given the strenuous nature of the scrambling on this route it is not such a good idea to encumber yourself with all the heavy gear needed for camping. The best option is to book a bed well in advance at the superbly situated Pen y Pass Youth Hostel (tel. 01286 870428), or try the more upmarket Pen y Gwryd Hotel (tel. 01286 870211) just to the east of the hostel along the road to Capel Curig.

gentler walking. The ridge is very narrow, and although straightforward enough, there is no easy escape once committed. The route then traverses the ridge of Crib y Ddysgl before finding a route down to Llanberis high above the Snowdon Railway.

Day One: Moel Eilio and the Summit of Wales

Start the walk from the youth hostel and head up-hill along the lane. The track soon turns towards the little valley holding Llyn Dwythwch and takes you around the long north-east ridge of Moel Eilio, the dome-shaped mountain that holds the view over the western side of Llanberis. A path turns off to the right and gains this ridge low down. Follow this path and make your way up the ridge to reach a fence high up on the slopes of **Moel Eilio**. Turn left along this and climb a stile to reach the bald top of the hill.

Moel Eilio translates as 'the supporting bare hill'. Its summit is marked by a huge ancient cairn and here you will find yourself 726m above sea level. The view of the main Snowdon range southwards are good, but it is the flatlands of Anglesey over the Menai Strait that draw the eye to the distant wart of Holyhead Mountain. Westwards the view takes in the Rivals, Yr Eifel, a fine range of small hills on the Lleyn Peninsular.

Turn south from the summit of Moel Eilio and cross a wall to pick up a good path that leads down to a col. Continue up the next bump, known as Foel Gron, then over a second bump on the same summit plateau. A deep col follows and the path climbs up over the next switchback to **Foel Goch**, a fine, grassy summit with a tiny cairn. Walk south from the summit and follow a fence down to a deep col at 467m by a gate through a stone wall.

Go through the gate and turn left immediately climbing gently along the long ridge of **Moel Cynghorion**. This is a superb little mountain with a big view over Llanberis and the dark face of Clogwyn Du'r Arddu of Snowdon.

Clogwyn Du'r Arddu, or Cloggy as it is universally known, is one of the most impressive crags in Britain, particularly for the hard men of rock climbing. Famous names from climbing history are interwoven with the classic climbs themselves, and those who have made their mark here include such greats as Menlove Edwards, Jack Longland, Joe Brown, Pete Crew and Jerry Moffatt.

Head south-east from the summit down to a col where you join the eroded Snowdon Ranger

The Snowdon Ranger Path starts by the shores of Llyn Cwellyn and provides one of the easiest, and certainly the oldest, track to the summit of Snowdon.

Path. Turn east up this track which climbs above the cliffs of Cloggy. ◄

The track is simple to follow and soon brings you out at the railway line that brings coach-loads of tourists up from Llanberis to the summit of **Snowdon**. Turn right along the track and follow the path up to the summit itself at 1085m.

> The top station of the Snowdon Mountain Railway, and the Snowdon Hotel grace the summit, which is just an over-priced café and gift shop. However, this is the place to buy that 'I've Climbed Snowdon' T-shirt that you've always wanted. This is the naff side of Snowdon; the crowds, the rubbish, and the holiday atmosphere. The summit itself is a huge unmistakable cairn with an OS trig pillar on the top. The true Welsh name of the summit is Yr Wyddfa, which means 'burial ground'. It originates from the old story that a giant called Rhita Gawr was slain here by King Arthur, who threw a pile of rocks over his dead body.

Y Lliwedd

Leaving the café (though horrible and over-priced, you can't help having a weak cup of tea or sending a postcard home), turn left outside the doors and follow the outside of the building around to the southern side. Pick up a broad path here dropping between a few rock pinnacles down to the south-west. After just a few hundred metres a large standing stone, the Finger Post, marks the top of a path dropping steeply off the ridge to the left. Follow this scree-covered path carefully, aiming down to a col, the Bwlch y Saethau, in a series of nasty zigzags.

> Bwlch y Saethau means 'pass of the arrows' and it is said that this is where King Arthur met his end. An old cairn here was supposed to be one of the many places where his body rests, but the cairn has long since gone, and there is no historical evidence to support this theory.

Cross the bwlch and pass around the right-hand side of a rocky knoll, picking up a good path that leads to a junction. Do not take the one on the right heading down into the valley as this will bring you down on the wrong side of the mountain. Instead, go straight ahead up the steep, rocky flank of **Y Lliwedd**. This gives some good scrambling, although quite easy, and offers plenty of options. For those wanting some exposure stay close to the top edge of the cliffs on the left, while for those wanting no more than a mountain walk, follow the paths to the right. They all lead to the summit of **Y Lliwedd**. ▸

There are three tops to this fine peak, the one to the west being the higher at 898m.

Continue along the crest to the next little summit, then down the rocks to the third, lower top of the mountain. Here the path becomes much more obvious and leads steeply down over rough crags and scree to the north. The gradient of the track eases just as it reaches the eastern tip of Llyn Llydaw where the main track up Snowdon is reached. This is the Miner's Track. Turn right along this and follow it to the large car park, information centre and youth hostel at **Pen y Pass**, where you should stay the night.

Day Two: The Traverse of Crib Goch and Criby Ddysgl

Begin by crossing the road from the hostel and making for the western-most corner of the car park. From here a good track takes you westwards around the rocky flanks of the hill to a little col at a stile. The track continues over the col, but to your right the steep ramparts of Crib Goch rise above the rough hillside. This is the route you will be taking. Turn westwards and climb easily at first to a steep wall immediately beneath the crest leading up to the east summit of **Crib Goch**. Right in the middle of this wall a groove can be climbed and leads to a corner where good holds lead onto the wall above. Step left around a spur, then upwards again up water-worn slabs to much easier scrambling. For those with a head for heights this is all very straightforward and is easily possible for the average hillwalker. Above lies more scary ground, but the most technical part is actually over. The ridge narrows above and leads to the fine East Summit of **Crib Goch**. Turn left here and scramble along the narrow crest. Some manage this by striding confidently over the very teeth of the crenellations, whereas many others sidle along on their bottoms. Which ever method you decide to use, don't worry about it, you will not be alone as this is the most popular ridge scramble in Britain. The ridge soon passes over the summit of **Crib Goch** at 923m, which usually goes by unnoticed. Then comes a big pillar of rock. Walk down to the left of this, and then scramble along ledges on its steep flank to an obvious notch between this first pillar and the next. This is very exposed, but the way onwards is easy. Climb out to the right of the second pillar from the notch, then head upwards on huge holds the size of buckets to the top of the pillar. An easy gully leads down off the pillar into the broad col of Bwlch Goch and the end of the Crib Goch traverse.

Walk westwards along the obvious path to the rocks rising to the summit of Crib y Ddysgl. From the toe of the buttress walk left for a few metres, then climb up right on

Scrambling around the second pinnacle on Crib Goch

a sloping series of ledges to a point above the steep rocks below. A pinnacle on the left has a gully to its immediate right and you should clamber up this to a step left at the top. Easy walking leads on to the summit of Crib y Ddysgl at 1065m.

Walk south-westwards along the track from the summit to reach the railway tracks at a finger post.

Without a doubt the most popular tourist attraction in Llanberis is the Snowdon Mountain Railway. This was opened in March 1896 after taking only 72 days to lay the track. On Easter Monday the first train made the ascent. All went well until it began chugging back down again. Somehow the line had become slightly buckled above the Clogwyn Station half way up, and as the train passed over this section the coaches automatically uncoupled themselves from the locomotive. The automatic hand brakes on the coaches stopped them safely, but the locomotive itself plunged into a ravine. The driver and fireman were lucky to escape uninjured, although two panicking passengers on the coaches jumped off before it had slowed to a halt and one died from his injuries. This first day of the railway saw the only major accident in its entire history.

Turn right along the track and walk down along the good path to **Clogwyn Station**. Here the footpath crosses the line, but for better views you should stay to the east of the railway and make your way out to the fine little summit of Llechog, overlooking the Pass of Llanberis. Continue down the rocky ridge running parallel to the railway, then begin to make your way towards it as you near Llanberis. The path is obvious and soon has you among the bright lights of this mountain town.

4 – The Moelwynion from Dolwyddelan

Total Distance:	43km
Daily Distances:	1) 21km 2) 14km
Maps:	OS Outdoor Leisure, sheets 17 and 18 *Snowdon and Conwy Valley* and *Snowdonia – Harlech and Bala*. The whole walk is on the OS Landranger sheet 115 *Snowdon and Caernarfon*.
Starting Point:	The railway station at Dolwyddelan, reached on the line from Llandudno Junction to Blaenau Ffestiniog. It is just off the A470(T) (grid ref. SH 738 521)

Area Summary: The Moelwynion, or Moelwyns as they are invariably known, are a rough group of high summits connected by broad ridges that form some of the wildest terrain in Snowdonia. In the southern half of the range much quarrying has gone on in the past, and in one or two places continues to be profitable to this day, but by and large the area is now quickly establishing itself as a fine place to explore on foot. The range is vaguely bounded to the east and south by the Lledr Valley and, over the Crimea Pass taken by the A470(T), the old mining town of Blaenau Ffestiniog. Boundaries to the west and north are more obvious, with the once tidal trench of the Aberglaslyn marking the former with the equally deep trench of the Nant Gwynant and Nantygwryd marking the northern boundary.

Walk Summary: A tough walk over surprisingly hard terrain, starting at Dolwyddelan in the Lledr Valley. The walk begins with a steep slog up arguably the best summit of the range, Moel Siabod, before crossing what few people realise is possibly the remotest country in this part

Transport: Trains run regularly between the coast at Llandudno Junction and Blaenau Ffestiniog and provide a convenient way of reaching Dolwyddelan. Drivers can turn off the A5 just before the turn for Betws-y-Coed and follow the A470(T) to Dolwyddelan.

Accommodation and supplies: There are loads of B&Bs and a campsite in Betws-y-Coed just a few miles north-east of the start. There are also plenty of shops there, including a good selection of outdoor-equipment shops. There are no shops along the route. In Dolwyddelan itself there is a small supermarket. For accommodation here try Bryn Tirion Farm (tel. 01690 750366) which has B&B, a campsite and a bunkhouse. This is just outside the village to the west, but for a bed in Dolwyddelan itself try the Elen's Castle Hotel (tel. 01690 750207).

Overnight Options: There is little choice here but to camp wild, and the route suggested makes use of the ground around Llyn Cwm Corsiog. Those looking for more comfort could try one of the B&Bs in Blaenau Ffestiniog.

of Snowdonia, the rough ground between Siabod and the northern outliers of the main part of the range, Ysgafell Wen. The terrain in between is hard going at times, but offers superb walking with big views of the Snowdon and Glyderau ranges to the north. The route continues into the main part of the range, taking in the lovely little summit of Cnicht before finding a spot to bed down for the night around the many high tarns that dot this landscape. Day Two continues with the peaks around the head of Cwmorthin before crossing the main road at the Crimea Pass and tackling the quieter summits of Moel Penamnen.

Day One: Over the Bald Hill of the Abbot

From the railway station walk across the bridge along the narrow road and follow it uphill to the main road junction in the centre of **Dolwyddelan**. Cross over and follow the lane almost opposite until it bends to the right.

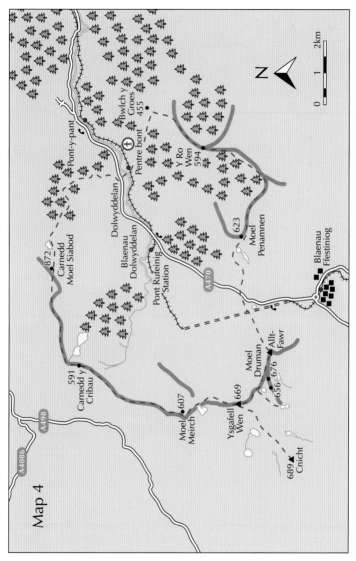

Map 4

N

0   1   2km

Bwlch y Croes 455

Pont-y-pant

Pentre bont

Y Ro Wen 594

Carnedd Moel Siabod 872

Dolwyddelan

Blaenau Dolwyddelan

Moel Penamnen 623

Blaenau Ffestiniog

Pont Rufeing Station

A470

Allt-Fawr

Carnedd y Cribau 591

Moel Meirch 607

Moel Druman 669

676
656

Ysgafell Wen 669

Cnicht 689

A4086

A498

Crossing the Moelwynion

Go around this bend and continue along this through Pen-y-gelli farm to where it becomes a track climbing uphill to the right of a low knoll. Here the track bears right, keeping above a shallow valley, and enters the forest. Follow the track to cross the Afon Ystumiau. This stream is the outflow of Llyn y Foel which nestles below the steep eastern face of the mountain. After leaving its banks for a short while, the path regains the side of it and you should follow the gushing waters up to the lake in the cwm above. ▶

From Llyn y Foel walk around the southern shore and ascend the pleasant rocky ridge known as Daiar Ddu which leads around the rim of the cirque holding the Llyn to the summit at 872m. The summit of **Moel Siabod**, the 'bald hill of the abbot' has a large cairn and an Ordnance Survey triangulation pillar standing atop a rocky little tor.

All other tracks from the summit lead down to Capel Curig, but ours heads off into the unknown across path-less terrain to the west. Head west from the summit down the ridge known as Moel Gîd where a vague path comes and goes as you descend. The ridge narrows and so becomes easier to follow as it drops to the Bwlch-y-maen above the twin lakes of Llynau Diwaunedd.

Careful navigation is needed now in anything but the best weather. Turn to the south and climb over the summit of **Carnedd y Cribau**, following the south-west ridge down off that summit to the low pass at Bwlch y Rhediad.

Looking north-west from the col you will see one of the finest pieces of mountain architecture in Britain, the Snowdon Horseshoe. Narrow ridges curve around the cwm holding Llyn Llydaw, culminating in the highest mountain in Britain south of the Scottish Highlands, Snowdon itself, at 1085m high. To the right of Snowdon lies the rocky, crenellated ridge of the twin summits of Crib Goch and Crib y Ddysgl, while to the left coming directly towards your vantage point is Y Lliwedd.

Just west of south the ground rises over a succession of knolls and dips via the broad ridge of Cerrig Cochion to the top of **Moel Meirch** at 607m. The summit is a fine little top, requiring an easy, short scramble from the western side to the tip of the peak itself. Descend from

W. P. Haskett Smith, who became known as the father of British Rock Climbing, wrote in 1836 that a few years previously a man had died on these slopes after becoming exhausted. He died during the night on the mountain and was later carried down to Capel Curig for burial there.

Moel Meirch

These three summits are connected by a vague ridge, the highest being the most southerly at 672m.

this fine little top to the northern tip of Llyn Edno, the pleasant tarn to the south. Walk around this on its eastern side and climb easily over rough grass and boulders to the three summits of **Ysgafell Wen**. A broken fence marks the way, and has a vague and sometimes boggy path alongside. ◄

From Ysgafell Wen the terrain is still difficult, both underfoot and in terms of navigation. Head just south of west to pick up an initially vague ridge line above Llyn yr Adar and Llyn y Biswall. Pass these two tarns on your right until the ridge becomes much more defined and a path appears underfoot leading along the ridge to the superb little summit of **Cnicht** at 689m. The summit is marked by a small cairn, but on such a well-defined summit it is superfluous.

Retrace your steps towards Ysgafell Wen but before reaching the domed summit, head off to the right across the head of Cwm Croesor to Llyn Cwm Corsiog. Camp here for the night.

Day Two: Allt-Fawr and East of the Crimea Pass

Starting the day high up in the mountains makes for an easy first hill, and although the terrain underfoot is quite rough and sometimes boggy, the route from your camp to the top of **Moel Druman** is straightforward and easily achieved. Walk around to the northern point of Lyn Cwm Corsiog and head northeast from there to the summit at 676 metres high. A fence leads off in the general direction of your next objective, **Allt-fawr**, away to the east and, although it doesn't take you right to the summit, it is a good initial guide. The summit of Allt-fawr at 698m stands on top of a low, rocky ridge on the eastern end overlooking the Gloddfa Ganol Slate Mines above Blaenau Ffestiniog.

From the summit, walk north to cross another vague, low ridge, then head north-east down onto a proper rib leading off the mountain with a faint path underfoot. At a little col, before you start to climb up again, the path branches and you should take the one on the right heading downhill to the tiny reservoir known as Llyn Iwerddon. Walk round to the dam and follow the small stream downhill to a flat platform with an airshaft in the middle. ▸

This airshaft serves the railway line running through the tunnel from Dolwyddelan through to Blaenau Ffestiniog.

Walk eastwards along the access track to the main road and the Bwlch y Gorddinan, better known as the Crimea Pass, the name of an inn which once stood there.

Cross the road and climb up the southern shoulder of Moel Farlwyd to a vague col known as Ffridd y Bwlch. Here turn north-east and climb to the top of this minor summit at 577m. Follow the ridge around to the east, dropping immediately to the next col just above Llynnau Barlwyd before climbing to the grassy top of **Moel Penamnen** at 623m. One kilometre to the east you will see the rough little mound of Foel-fras, and this is your next objective. Once there, a fence line is picked up and you should follow this around to the south then to the east, keeping to the top edge of the cwm that holds the vast forestry plantations that fill Cwm Penamnen to the north. At the foot of this cwm lies Dolwyddelan, but to reach it you must traverse the eastern ridge of the cwm over Y Ro Wen.

Follow the fence around the cwm, and once you are heading in a northerly direction leave it behind and

Allt-fawr

climb up the easy-angled south ridge of **Y Ro Wen** to the summit cairn at 594m. To the east from this summit lies another forested valley, Glascwm, and now from the top you should follow the upper edge of this cwm along the long north-eastern ridge of Y Ro Wen and down to the major pass at Bwlch y Groes. Here an ancient coach road is picked up that goes over the pass from Penmachno in the east to Dolwyddelan in the north-west. Turn left down and off the pass, and following a stream, the Afon Bwlch y Groes, down to a forest edge, you should walk on a path to Pentre-bont and the railway station at **Dolwyddelan**.

5 – The Moel Hebog Hills and Nantlle Ridges: The Mountains of Eifionydd

Total Distance:	31km
Daily Distances:	1) 12km 2) 19km
Maps:	OS Outdoor Leisure, sheet 17 *Snowdon and Conwy Valley*
Starting Point:	The telephone box in Cwm Pennant, where there are also spaces to park. Cwm Pennant is reached from various minor roads off the A487(T) from Porthmadog to Caernarfon. Grid ref. SH 532 454

Area Summary: The mountains of Eifionydd are sandwiched between the two roads leading from Porthmadog to Caernarfon, the A487(T) to the west and the A4085 to the east. The main summits of these mountains are contained within two long ridges forming roughly a letter 'T', with one of the finest of these summits, Trum y Ddysgl, at the point where the two ridges meet. There are some spectacular mountains in these two main ranges, and this walk takes in all the main summits of Eifionydd.

Walk Summary: An easy walk with well-defined paths and tracks once on the heights. These hills are more usually tackled from the east from Beddgelert or Rhyd Ddu where many people walking in this range will choose to stay. However, western approaches are superb, though unfrequented, and are much better for those with a tendency to want to explore beautiful mountain terrain rather than just bag the peaks. The walk starts out by finding a devious way up arguably the best peak in the range, Moel Hebog, from Cwm Llefrith, then traverses the classic 'Hebog Ridge' over the two remaining peaks of the range, Moel yr Ogof and Moel Lefn. After a descent to the low col at Bwlch-y-ddwy-elor, forest tracks lead down to Rhyd Ddu and a short section of road walking leads to the Snowdon Ranger Youth Hostel. Day Two starts with the short return along the road to Rhyd Ddu from where the other main ridge of this range is tackled. Y Garn is the first summit of the 'Nantlle Ridge', and from there the fantastic switchback ridge continues over Trum y Ddysgl, Mynydd Tal-y-mignedd, Craig Cwm Silyn and Garnedd Goch before walking on to the lower summit of Mynydd Graig Goch. A descent is then made down Cwm Ciprwth back into Cwm Pennant.

Transport: A car is essential to reach the start, as there is no public transport in Cwm Pennant.

Accommodation and supplies: Again, there is nothing in Cwm Pennant itself, but most people will be happy staying in Beddgelert and driving around from there for the start of this walk. Hotels and guesthouses worth checking out in Beddgelert are Ael-y-Bryn on Caernarfon Road (tel. 01766 890310) and Plas Colwyn by the bridge (tel. 01766 890458). There are two good campsites just outside Beddgelert, the better one being the Forestry Commission campsite just north of the village (tel. 01766 890288), while Cae Du Camp Site just east of the village (tel. 01766 890595) is more basic. There is a bunkhouse at Bryn Dinas just beyond Cae Du heading east (tel. 01766 890234). Beddgelert has shops and a small supermarket, as does the Forestry Commission campsite. North of Beddgelert at Rhyd Du is the Cwellyn Arms which has accommodation including B&B, bunkhouse and camping nearby (tel. 01766 890321).

Overnight Options: This particular walk is suitable for those new to backpacking, who may not necessarily have all of the equipment needed to camp out on the mountains. For this reason it is recommended that you stay overnight at either the Snowdon Ranger Youth Hostel (tel. 01286 650391) or at the B&B, bunkhouse, or campsite at the Cwellyn Arms as mentioned above.

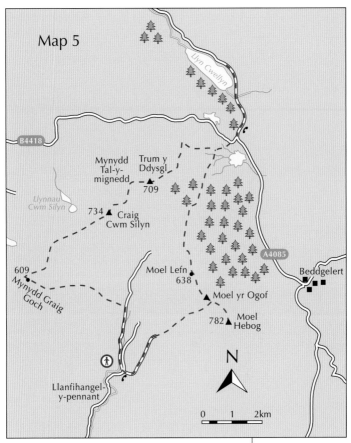

Day One: The Hebog Ridge from Cwm Pennant

Start by walking east from the junction by the telephone box. Follow the road until it swings left, and then take the public footpath at the bend on the right, climbing gently up to a junction of paths. Take the one on the left and continue uphill alongside a stream. Climb eastwards until you reach the boundary of open hillside and continue over rough terrain until the long south-west ridge of Moel Hebog is reached low down. Pick a way through the walls and fences and climb up this south-west ridge to the summit of **Moel Hebog** at 782m.

> Beneath the eastern face Moel Hebog's top lie the cliffs of Y Diffwys. The story goes that Owain Glyndŵr swam across the river in the valley to the east when he was fleeing from his armed pursuers. He cleared the rushing waters of the Afon Glaslyn at Nantmor, which was tidal and much wider in those days, then continued to climb the mountain beyond, still with the English in hot pursuit. Only the summit cliffs of Moel Hebog looked like stopping him but then he found a chimney cutting through the difficult rocks and climbed it to the top. The current rock climber's guidebook points out in prose, typical of old mountaineering records, that 'A strong English party failed to follow!' Owain then made his way over to a cave on the next mountain, Moel yr Ogof, where he hid away for the next six months.

The summit of Moel Hebog is obvious, marked as it is by a large cairn, an Ordnance Survey triangulation pillar, and a stone wall. To continue, turn north-west alongside the stone wall and follow it steeply downhill to a rocky little col known as Bwlch Meillionen. Ahead rises **Moel yr Ogof**. ◄

The path leads uphill through a rocky cleft, and although steep throughout, you will soon find yourself heading towards the summit cairn atop its little rocky knoll at 655m.

Continue north-westwards from the summit, down to a grassy col with odd bits of scree showing, then up to the uninteresting summit of **Moel Lefn** at 638m. The route from the summit seems obvious initially as you head off northwards down the ridge. Follow the path throughout as there are crags and rough heathery ground

The cave where Owain Glyndŵr hid from the English is around to the right overlooking the Beddgelert Forest, but it is not recommended as a route for walkers.

all around lower down. The path leads downhill beside a large rock slab with a big quartz band running through it, then on down to the bouldery col known locally as Bwlch Cwm-trwsgl.

Ahead, as you descend to the bwlch, is the low though very rough ridge of Y Garn which you should climb via a broad boulder-strewn gully to its rocky top. Follow the ridge east of north for a short way to the summit at 452m, and then continue along the ridge for a further 300m until it is possible to drop off the ridge to the west down to a stone wall. Just along the wall you will see a track coming up out of Cwm Pennant to the left and heading into the Beddgelert Forest to the right. Make for this track along the side of the wall, reaching it at a gateway.

From the gate turn right and follow the good track downhill through the forest in a north-easterly direction. Pass to the left of a quarry that is almost hidden in the trees, then down on the narrowing path to join a good forestry track. Turn right here, then left almost immediately continuing straight ahead at the next junction on the left until you drop down to a stream. Ignore the junction to the right, and crossing the stream follow a fire

Y Garn

break with a path running along it northwards until you emerge onto the open hillside on the eastern ridge of Mynydd Drws-y-coed.

The track is now very obvious, contouring around the eastern flank of this hill and eventually descending to a ladder stile above Llyn-y-Gader. Follow the track around to the right through strong growing hard rushes and out to the B4418, just outside Rhyd Ddu village. Turn right and follow the road into the village. The Cwellyn Arms pub is on the junction on the right, and will sort you out with accommodation if you have booked to stay there. Those heading for the Snowdon Ranger Youth Hostel should turn left at the junction and follow the main road northwards for 3km where you will find the hostel on the right, just opposite Llyn Cwellyn.

Day Two: The Nantlle Ridge

Start the day by retracing your steps from Rhyd Ddu village. Walk along the road to the point where the bridleway branches off to the left at the bend on the B4418, and follow the track around and up to the ladder stile above Llyn-y-Gader. Now ignore the track going across the hillside that you came down on last night, and instead

Nantlle Ridge

climb up the good path heading straight for the summit of Y Garn high above. The way is very steep, but it offers a direct route onto the tops and to the start of the Nantlle Ridge traverse.

High up on the summit plateau of Y Garn you reach a stone wall and the summit cairn stands just beyond at 633m.

The summit of Y Garn offers one of the best view-points in Snowdonia. Northwards rise the broken red cliffs of Craig y Bera on the flanks of Mynydd Mawr across the Nantlle valley, while to the east the whole of the Snowdon massif is stretched out. Southwards the view takes in the Hebog hills that you traversed yesterday, and beyond, in the gap between Hebog and Snowdon you can see the Moelwyns and the Rhinogs. On a really clear day you can just pick out the Cadair Idris peaks, Arenigs, Arans and even Plynlimon. South-westwards the view is dominated by the continuation of this walk, the magnificent Nantlle Ridge Traverse.

Follow the wall south-westwards to a rocky col. The stark ridge of Mynydd Drws-y-coed rears up in front and some easy scrambling leads up the very crest of this and onto the fine summit by a stile. The top at 695m high lies right on the edge of the huge drop into the cwm to the north. ▸

Follow the obvious ridge down to the south-west from the summit, and at the col a good path will be picked up. Follow this for a short way, but keep an eye out for a very faint path on the right which leaves the main one and climbs up to the summit of **Trum y Ddysgl** along its south ridge. Do not stick to the main path as it bypasses the summit and you'll miss half the fun! The summit of Trum y Ddysgl lies at 709m at the north-eastern end of a ridge and is marked by a few stones as a cairn.

Mynydd Drws-y-coed translates into English literally as 'mountain at the door to the wood'.

Mynydd Tal-y-mignedd means 'mountain at the end of the bog'. The obelisk was built by quarrymen to commemorate the Diamond Jubilee of Queen Victoria.

From the summit head along the ridge to its south-western top then pick a way down to the col to west. A little rocky niche leads onto the col before an easy climb up grassy slopes takes you to a wall and the large obelisk on **Mynydd Tal-y-mignedd's** summit at 653m. ◄

From the summit obelisk a fence leads over boggy ground to the south, and you should follow this off the ridge until it turns right and goes down to a col via some loose shale slopes. Walk down these slopes, keeping left where the path seems to have a junction at the top of the shale. The way straight ahead is steeper and looser.

Once down on the col at Bwlch Dros-bern a great buttress of rock will be seen rising up above you on the other side. This is the way onto the next summit, **Craig Cwm Silyn**. There is a rather stiff scramble straight up the face of this buttress, but for those carrying full backpacks this cannot be recommended. Where the path rises towards the first of the rock steps above the col, another fainter path will be seen heading over to the right. Follow this to where it outflanks the buttress in short zigzags and leads easily onto a scree slope high up just below the summit. The path improves and takes you easily to the summit cairn at 734m. ◄

Craig Cwm Silyn translates as the 'crag above the Silyn valley'. It is a fine viewpoint on a good day. You can see over Anglesey to the north, the Rivals to the west, the Lleyn Peninsular to the south-west and the Snowdon range to the east.

Walk west from the summit, passing three ruined towers on the way over to a rocky knoll overlooking the awesome drop into Cwm Silyn to the north of the ridge. Handrail around the rim of the cwm until you reach a wall which takes you all the way to the top of the next summit, Garnedd Goch at 700m.

Continue south-west, then south down to the col at Bwlch Cwmdulyn where a public footpath will be picked up. This can be followed down to a little knoll at 475m to the south-east, then down the broad cwm beneath Graig-lwyd to a good track above Braich-garw. Turn eastwards along this track and follow the path on the east of the stream down to the Moelfre Quarries above Pont Gyfyng. Cross the bridge onto the public road and turn left, following the road to the telephone box where your car is parked.

6 – The Clwydian Range from Ruthin

Total Distance:	47km
Daily Distances:	1) 24km 2) 23km
Maps:	OS Explorer, sheet 256 *Wrexham and Llangollen*
Starting Point:	St Peter's Square in the centre of Ruthin. Grid Ref. SJ 123 583

Area Summary: A very quiet area in terms of numbers of hillwalkers likely to be seen along the route. The Clwydian range forms a long ridge running north to south, from the North Wales coast down to the flatter moorlands around Llangollen.

Walk Summary: A tough route over surprisingly hard terrain. The walk soon leaves Ruthin behind as it makes

Transport:	Buses run from Mold, Corwen and Denbigh and all stop on Market Street in Ruthin. Call the tourist office for bus details (tel. 01824 703992).
Accommodation and supplies:	There is no shortage of accommodation in Ruthin. Try the Castle Hotel on St Peter's Square (tel. 01824 70479) or Gorffwystfa B&B on Castle Street (tel. 01824 702748). The tourist office can advise on other options (tel. 01824 703992). There are plenty of shops in Ruthin, and some good cafes and restaurants too.
Overnight Options:	There are plenty of options in Llangollen, including the youth hostel (tel. 01978 860919) and Mile End Mill Bunkhouse (tel. 01978 869043) for those looking for a simple roof over their heads, or try The Royal Hotel (tel. 01978 860202), Jonkers (tel. 01978 861158), Gales (tel. 01978 860089) or Hafren (tel. 01978 860939) for something a bit more comfortable. Plenty of shops, cafés and restaurants in the town itself for food or beer.

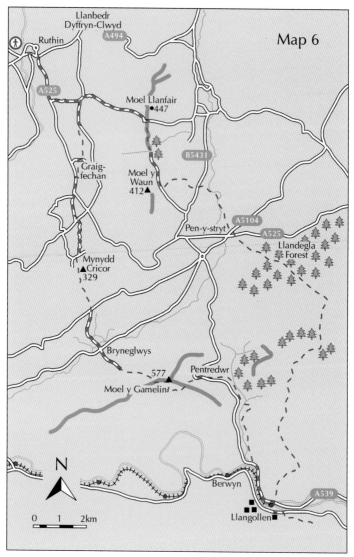

Map 6

Llanbedr
Dyffryn-Clwyd

Ruthin

A494

A525

Moel Llanfair
●447

Graig-
fechan

B5431

Moel y
Waun
412▲

Pen-y-stryt

A5104

A525

Llandegla
Forest

Mynydd
▲Cricor
329

Bryneglwys

577▲

Pentredwr

Moel y Gamelin

N

0   1   2km

Berwyn

A539

Llangollen

for the spine of the Clwydian range, just south of Moel Gyw. Here the walk picks up the line taken by the Offa's Dyke Path National Trail, following it southwards all the way to Tan-y-castell, just above Llangollen where you will spend the night. Day Two follows rights of way over the fantastic heathery ridge of Maesyrychen Mountain before continuing northwards along farm tracks back to Ruthin. The route is fairly easy to follow, but care should be taken in finding the correct paths and tracks to take in an area where there is a preponderance of likely looking ways.

Day One: Along the Offa's Dyke Path

Start by walking east from St Peter's Square in **Ruthin**, then bear right at the junction and follow the A525 south, until just clear of the last houses in the town. Here a public footpath sign points diagonally across a field to the left of the road. Follow this path out to a minor road and turn left along this, passing The Firs on the left and walking on to a junction with the B5429. Turn left along this B-road for 200m, then right onto another minor road. Follow this lane around a sharp bend to the right, then soon after take the even narrower lane on the left that climbs up gently towards the farm at Sinet. Just before Sinet the lane turns east and climbs steeply uphill alongside a wooded gully with a stream flowing along its bottom. Follow this lane up to Bryn-isaf Farm and continue uphill along the track to where it gains the ridge of the Clwydian Range at Moel Llech. Here you join the Offa's Dyke Path National Trail.

King Offa of Mercia had the massive earthwork now known as Offa's Dyke created in the eighth century as a demarcation line between his own land, which stretched right across much of central England, and that of Wales. Even in George Borrow's classic book, *Wild Wales*, he noted that 'it was customary for the ▸

◄ English to cut off the ears of every Welshman who was found to the east of the dyke, and for the Welsh to hang every Englishman whom they found to the west of it'. Today the England–Wales border criss-crosses the dyke many times, although the basic line of the boundary has remained very close to the original. In 1971 a long-distance footpath was created to follow the line of the dyke as closely as was possible. This is a superb walk of 117 miles running from Prestatyn on the north Clwyd coast to Sedbury Cliffs near Chepstow in Gwent.

Walk south along the Offa's Dyke Path, climbing very steeply up to a col between the two minor summits of Moel y Plâs, then down and across the head of a broad cwm. Follow the Path over the south ridge of Moel y Plâs, then south to the edge of the forest of Nurse Fawr where a radio mast will be seen. There is a good track running along the outside of the forest and you should follow this southwards to emerge at a minor road. Continue southwards, now along the road, for 600m to a point where the Offa's Dyke Path turns sharp left at Tyddyn-tlodion. Follow the Path eastwards downhill past the farm, and alongside field edges and out to a road near St Garmon's Well.

Cross straight over the road and pass between cave entrances before heading south-eastwards across boggy meadows, then south into the village of Llandegla. Walk south along the main street to the junction with the A5104 and cross straight over this. The minor road you are on turns to the left, and just around the bend the Offa's Dyke Path takes a turn off the road to the right before coming to the A525. Over the main road and slightly to the left the Offa's Dyke Path continues and you should follow it down to cross a stream before following field boundaries southeastwards to a little lane at Hafod Bilston. Turn right towards the farm, then left just beyond the farm buildings, entering the woodlands of

Llandegla Forest beside a little stream in a gully. Climb up through the forest on the north bank of the stream, following the path throughout as it climbs up to the southeast and eventually emerges from the trees onto the open moorland on the north-east ridge of Cyrn-y-Brain. This hill can be seen off to your right as you come out of the forest. Stay on the track as it heads southeastwards across the open moorland. ▸

The track dips to cross a stream, then soon brings you to a narrow road high on the moorland. Turn right along the road and follow it southwards to where it enters a forest at a cattle grid. Continue along the road to where it takes a very sharp bend to the right at a narrow gully known as World's End. Walk around the bend but look for a public footpath sign on the left almost immediately. This climbs up through the trees to Craig yr Adar where you will find yourself walking along beneath wonderful outcrops of glowing white limestone. The Offa's Dyke Path, which you are still following, contours high above the valley on your right to a water-washed gully above Rock Farm, and here you should follow the path down to a narrow lane at the farm itself. Turn southwards along the lane, bearing left at the first junction and continuing

Look out for red grouse as you walk across these moorlands. They are common hereabouts and are kept as a game bird. Grouse live on the young shoots of heather; patches of the ling, bell and cross-leaved heathers that grow here are burnt on a rotational basis to provide fresh growths every year.

Llangollen Moors

until you reach Tan-y-castell farm. A public footpath leads south-west from the road, then passes around the northern side of a dome-shaped hill with the ramparts of Castell Dinas Bran on its top. Continue around the foot of this hill to Tirionfa, and then pick up a good track heading south for the bridge over the River Dee in **Llangollen**. There are plenty of overnight options around either side of the bridge, but those heading for the youth hostel should cross over and climb uphill to the T-junction. Turn left here, then right along Ty'n-dwr Road which leads to the hostel after 2km.

Day Two: Maesyrychen Mountain

Wherever you slept the night, start the day by returning to the bridge over the River Dee in the centre of Llangollen. Walk over to the north side, turn left along the A542, heading westwards, and follow this on its northern side past the Royal International Pavilion.

The Royal International Pavilion is the venue for the Llangollen International Music Eisteddfod which takes place during the second week of July each year. Unlike the National Eisteddfod held at various locations throughout the Principality, the Llangollen Eisteddfod draws performers from around the World, and comes billed as 'The World's Greatest Folk Festival'.

Valle Cruces Abbey was founded in 1201 and was one of the last Cistercian foundations in Wales to be established, and was the first Gothic abbey in Britain.

Walk on past the Pavilion and continue along the road for over a kilometre until it begins to bend sharply to the left. At this point a minor road turns off to the right, and just beyond this a public footpath also leaves the main road on the right. Take this footpath northwards towards the Valle Crucis Abbey. ◄

The Abbey itself lies just over the Eglwyseg River to the west, and you can cross over to have a look around, but the walk continues in a northerly direction along the eastern bank. Walk through to Abbey Cottage, and then climb uphill on the right to enter a wood. The path here bears left, heading northwards again as it contours around the steep-sided hill to Hendre. Just beyond the farm at Hendre the path splits, and you should take the one on the left heading downhill to a little road. Turn left along the road and cross the bridge over the river. The road takes you steeply uphill and after 150m a public bridleway turns off left, leading you around the hillside and out onto another public road. Turn right along this and follow it northwards again to **Pentre-dwr**. Here turn left off the road onto a public footpath just beyond the chapel and follow the south bank of a tiny stream up the valley of Oernant.

There is a main road at the top of this valley, the A542 again, and you should cross this to the left and follow a narrow path up to the old quarries to the south-west. Walk through the quarries and up to cross a spur of Maesyrychen Mountain, contouring around it's southern slopes through deep heather and moorland grasses to a little col immediately south of the summit of Moel y Gamelin.

Walk north-west from the col down to a much broader col at a junction of paths between the two summits of **Moel y Gamelin** and Moel y Gaer. Pick up the bulldozed track heading north-west from the col and around the northern slopes of Moel y Gaer, eventually reaching the minor road at Plas-newydd at a junction. Ignore the lanes to right and left and go straight ahead down the hill and out to the main road, the A5104. Cross straight over this and continue along the minor lane to Ty'n-y-ffordd at another crossroads. Take the good track straight ahead again, climbing steeply up to the farmstead at Fron Goch Isa and continuing from here to the north along the track that brings you out at another minor road at spot height 359m. From the lane a public footpath leads downhill almost opposite, passing Castell Fury on its way to Tan-y-graig at another lane. Bear left along the lane and look immediately for the continuation of this footpath on the right, crossing the head of a stream as it goes over a nose then down into a valley on the other side where you should cross another stream in a narrow conifer wood. Climb out of the wood and head north-west to gain another lane, turning left along this past Cricor. At a sharp bend left a public bridleway follows a good track on the right and you should take this to Bryn Aur. Here the tracks split and you should take the main one on the left heading downhill through pastures to emerge through woodland at Faenol before taking the farm's drive out to the B5429. Turn left along the road, then right at a junction, walking along the quiet lane to come to a junction with the A525. Here turn left and walk along this main road for 600m until another lane comes in on the right. Take this, then after 150m look for a public footpath on the left that leads via Capel-y-fferm to Glan-yr-afon and on northwards through Melin Garth-Gynan to Garthgynan. From here follow the driveway out to the B5429 where you should turn left, northwards, and then left again at a crossroads of minor lanes. After 75m this lane takes a sharp left, and at this point a public footpath heads off north-westwards. Take this to another lane where you turn left then right after 200m, following a public footpath to Cantabra Farm on the southern outskirts of Ruthin. Turn right along the A525 to reach the centre of Ruthin and the end of this walk.

7 – The Rhinog Traverse

Total Distance:	36km
Daily Distances:	1) 19km 2) 17km
Maps:	OS Outdoor Leisure, sheet 18. *Snowdonia Harlech and Bala*
Starting Point:	The small car park at Llechfraith, grid ref. SH 667 197. Head north off the A496 at Bontddu between Dolgellau and Barmouth. After 1km, just before a bridge leads over a stream, park near the telephone box.

Area Summary: The Rhinogs form what is surely the roughest and perhaps wildest mountain mass in Wales. That said, it is a neat range running fairly smoothly south

Transport:	Buses running between Dolgellau and Harlech around the coastal road stop at Bontddu, from where you will have to walk up the road to Llechfraith.
Accommodation and supplies:	There are loads of B&Bs in Barmouth and Dolgellau. Try the Wavecrest Hotel on Marine Drive in Barmouth (tel. 01341 280330), or the basic Ivy House Hotel in Dolgellau (tel. 01341 422535). Better by far is Bryn yr Odyn in Dolgellau up off the Cadair Idris road (tel. 01341 423470). There is always the Caban Cader Idris bunkhouse just outside Dolgellau (tel. 01248 600478), or you could camp at Vanner Abbey Farm (tel. 01341 422854). There are shops in both Barmouth and Dolgellau, but none on the route itself.
Overnight Options:	There is a basic campsite in Cwm Bychan which is ideally situated for an overnight stay on this walk, grid ref. SH 646 314.

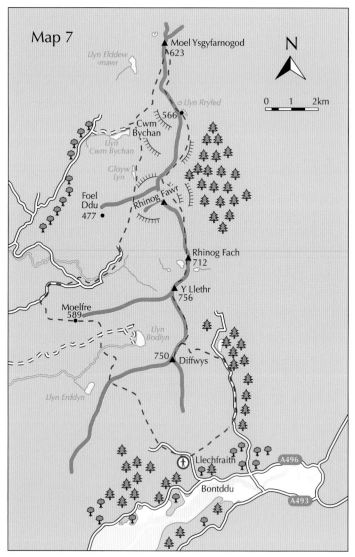

Map 7

N

0   1   2km

Moel Ysgyfarnogod
623

Llyn Elddew
-mawr

Llyn Rryfed

566
Cwm
Bychan

Llyn
Cwm Bychan

Gloyw
Lyn

Foel
Ddu
477

Rhinog Fawr

Rhinog Fach
712

Y Llethr
756

Moelfre
589

Llyn
Bodlyn

750   Diffwys

Llyn Erddyn

Llechfraith

Bontddu

A496

A493

to north from the Afon Mawddach Estuary near Dolgellau to the Vale of Ffestiniog. The A470(T) cuts the range off from the Arenigs to the east, while the west coast forms a more natural barrier to the west.

Walk Summary: A tough walk over hard terrain, following the classic ridge traverse of the main peaks of the Rhinog range. Although not a particularly long walk in itself, the ground underfoot is nowhere easy making for hard going. The route leads up the two most southerly peaks of the range, Diffwys and Y Llethr, which also happen to be the highest summits of the Rhinogs. Here the going is not too difficult, being mainly over bouldery grass slopes, but once you head north from Y Llethr knee-deep heather cloaks the slopes all around and rocky ribs of the mountain mass poke out, threatening to twist ankles and making for a very hard walk over to Cwm Bychan. The second day is slightly easier, keeping off the main ridge for the best part. However, there is still much climbing involved before you regain your car at Llechfraith.

Day One: The Rhinog Traverse

Navigationally the start of this walk is probably the hardest part of the route. Walk down to the bridge over the stream to the north of the small car park and take the track, a public footpath, on the right. This leads above the stream to the farm at Ty'n-y-cornel from where you should continue heading north-east through the spoils and deposits of the old Clogau mine. Continue over to a broad grassy col from where a series of little marker posts lead northwards to a corner of the forest cloaking the slopes of Cwm Mynach over to the east. The footpath continues just east of north through the forest into the cwm itself where it brings you out near the end of the road that runs up the valley to Blaen-cwm-mynach.

Turn left and head northwards along the road for a short way until it becomes a track at a junction. Go left here and continue northwards through the forest. ▸

Look out for siskin, crossbills, redpolls, and other finches here as this is one of the best places in North Wales for seeing such fantastic birdlife.

73

This raised bed of cobbles formed the tramway for the old manganese and gold mines that covered the hills around Cwm Mynach.

The walk continues along this track for just under 2km. At one point a large felled area will be seen on the left with the rocky mass of Y Garn rising across the cwm to the right. Just beyond this point, where the track enters the forest again you will see a little path on the left leading along a rocky causeway to the west. ◄

Follow the track through the trees and out onto the open heathery hillside. Continue along it and climb steadily uphill through rough ground to a flat traverse across the tramway to the south-west. Beyond a rocky spur falling from the south-east ridge of Y Llethr the going becomes much steeper and takes you northwards up to the head of Cwm Llechen.

This 6 foot high stone wall traverses the whole of the southern half of the main Rhinogs ridge and is an infallible guide in poor visibility. This magnificent structure, which in some parts of the Rhinogs range reaches a height of 8 feet, was built by French prisoners during the Napoleonic Wars.

There is a good population of feral goats on the Rhinogs and this cwm is one of the best places to find them. They are not truly wild as many people believe, but are in fact descended from the domestic goats that were kept by the local people who lived up in the hills in the past. In many areas of Wales they are deliberately encouraged by the farmers who value their habit of eating vegetation on the crags. This stops the sheep venturing onto terrain that would be dangerous for them.

Climb up to the head of Cwm Llechen to reach a high stone wall between the summit of Diffwys and Crib-y-rhiw. ◄

From the col our route goes northwards along the ridge, but it would be a real shame not to include the summit of **Diffwys**. Turn left along the south side of the wall and follow it for ½km to the summit trig pillar perched in a magnificent position, atop a line of cliffs falling away steeply to the east. ◄

The summit of Diffwys is at 750m above sea level. The name Diffwys translates as 'the precipice'.

Retrace your steps along the side of the wall to the col at the head of Cwm Llechen, then climb the wall using the ladder stile and follow the path north-eastwards around the north side of a subsidiary little knoll before picking up the wall again and following it in a northerly direction. This passes by some small pools on the left, just above the much bigger Llyn Dulyn, and then starts to climb to the next summit along the ridge, Crib-y-rhiw. This is really just another subsidiary peak of the much bigger Y Llethr which lies just to the north – you should pass over the rocky tops of Crib-y-rhiw and on to the climb up **Y Llethr**. A little inconspicuous cairn marks the highest point at the southern end of the long grassy ridge which forms the top of 'the Slope' at 756m.

Descending Y Garn

Here the going changes to much rough terrain. You leave the easy grass slopes behind and start to head into the wilds of the Rhinogs. Geologists know the Rhinogs as the Harlech Dome from the great beds of gritstone and sandstone which are exposed throughout the range and continue to fall well below the outcropping rocks of the other nearby mountain ranges in Snowdonia. The rocks of the Harlech Dome lie far beneath Snowdon itself, although the rocks here are probably a hundred million years younger than the Ordovician summits of the main Snowdon range.

Continue from the summit of Y Llethr by following the wall again north-eastwards, easily at first, then more steeply down rough scree-covered slopes to a narrow col above the wild and dramatic Llyn Hywel. Ahead the bouldery slopes of **Rhinog Fach** loom, dark and threatening. Climb these slopes beside the wall at first, then veering off to the left slightly to gain the summit at 712m.

A rough and not always obvious path leaves the summit northwards, passing over many short crags and rocky steps before descending to the crag-girt col at Bwlch Drws-Arduddwy. Aim for the highest point of the bwlch by a cairn, then pick up a very vague path that climbs the broad eastern flank of **Rhinog Fawr**. This seems to lead far away from the summit itself, but then, almost as an afterthought, veers to the west and brings the summit trig pillar out in front at 720m.

Leave the summit of Rhinog Fawr to the north of west, passing around broken crags before heading back to the north-east to the eastern side of Llyn Du. Continue north-eastwards from the Llyn, aiming for the top of the Roman Steps.

These steps, now well worked after the passage of thousands of feet over the centuries, are indeed very old, but are probably not Roman. The pass was once an important trade route between Harlech and Bala, and in medieval times was used as the main line of communications between Harlech Castle and London. On the Cwm Bychan side, to the west, the hundreds of stone flag steps can still be seen and walked upon to this day.

If you feel you are by now starting to flag a little, you can easily reach the small campsite in Cwm Bychan to the west by following the Roman Steps down off the ridge in that direction. However, our route continues northwards for a further 3km into what have been called the Celtic Badlands. This is very rough country indeed. Walk north-east from the top of the Roman Steps to the eastern side of Llyn Morwinion, then climb eastwards to gain the rocky ridge at spot height 518m. Undulating ground continues northwards over rock-scarred slopes, clad in thick heather, to Craig Wion's summit at 566m, then off to the north-west and down to a footpath leading over the mountains from the south-west to the north-east. Turn left along this footpath and descend into the very head of **Cwm Bychan**, emerging on a minor road half way along the north side of Llyn Cwm Bychan. Turn left along the road and walk to the road end and the little campsite where you will pitch your tent for the night.

Day Two: Cwm Nantcol and Moelfre

Start the day by heading south through the lovely woods around the head of Cwm Bychan and up the Roman Steps path. At the top end of the wood the Roman Steps head off to the south-east, whereas your path continues southwards alongside a stone wall. From the corner of the wall head south-west for the northern tip of the lonely Gloyw Lyn, walking clockwise around this lovely expanse to the southern shore. From this point a very faint footpath heads south across much rough and open ground, rising gently over the western ridge of Rhinog Fawr. Aim between two sheepfolds shown on the 1:25,000 map, then descend into the head of Cwm Nantcol to the road end at Maes-y-garnedd. Follow the track into the farm itself, and then pick up a public footpath along

Moelfre

the southern side of a small tributary stream of the Afon Cwmnantcol, crossing it at one point as you head down stream to Pont Cerrig.

Turn left over the bridge and take the public footpath on the right, heading along the southern bank of the Afon Cwmnantcol to Glan-rhaidr. Here head out southwards onto a minor lane and turn right for the farmstead at Hendre-waelod. Leave the road here and take the public footpath to the south of the farm buildings, climbing gently across the slopes to Gelli-bant where you meet another narrow lane. Turn west along this, climbing at first, then veering round to the south at a small car park. Five hundred metres beyond the car park look for a public footpath sign on the left. Follow this southwards for 1km, to a point where the track underfoot starts to climb up the hill on the left rather than just contouring around its slopes. Follow this track uphill to a fence, cross over this then follow it uphill eastwards to the summit of **Moelfre**.

Moelfre is a fantastic viewpoint for viewing the rest of the Rhinogs. Look eastwards into the rough bounds and cwms of Diffwys, Y Llethr, Rhinog Fach and Rhinog Fawr. Northwards you can see into the Moelwyns and Snowdon ranges, while southwards across the Mawddach Estuary the peaks of Cadair Idris dominate the view. Westwards, Cardigan Bay draws the eye away to the possibility of views of Ireland on a clear day.

Head east from the summit of Moelfre to a point on the lower ridge, just above the col that connects Moelfre to Y Llethr, where a public bridleway is shown on the map crossing the ridge from north to south. Turn southwards along this and descend, steeply at first, to Pont-Scethin which crosses the Afon Ysgethin, the outflow of Llyn Bodlyn Reservoir.

Crossing Pont-Scethin two paths head off away from the stream on its southern side. Take the one going south-eastwards, climbing steeply up and around the vast, craggy slopes of Craig y Grut, the long south-west ridge of Diffwys climbed yesterday. Go eastwards, then southwards around these crags in a huge zigzag, eventually aiming for the cairn at spot height 572m, high on the ridge.

Turn left along the ridge, heading eastwards back towards Diffwys, then pick up a track on the right after 400m. This track will take you down the superb ridge known as Braich to the road head at Banc-y-Frân. Turn eastwards and walk down the road to your car just over the bridge at **Llechfraith**.

Crossing the broad col between Moelfre and Y Llethr

8 – The Mountains of Arenig from Llyn Tegid

Total Distance:	77km
Daily Distances:	1) 33km 2) 23km 3) 21km
Maps:	OS Landranger, sheets 124 *Dolgellau and Porthmadog* and 125 *Bala and Lake Vyrnwy, Berwyn*
Starting Point:	The Bala railway station car park on the Bala Lake Railway at grid ref. SH 930 350
Finishing Point:	The Llanuwchllyn railway station car park on the Bala Lake Railway at grid ref. SH 881 300

Area Summary: The Arenigs are one of the wildest and most scattered mountain ranges in Wales. They are split roughly into three separate groups: the northern Arenigs, comprising Arenig Fach, Carnedd y Filiast and Foel Goch; the central Arenigs where the highest peaks are clustered – Arenig Fawr and Moel Llyfnant; and the southern Arenigs of Rhobell Fawr and Dduallt. The range is basically triangular in shape, with the A494(T) from Bala to Dolgellau forming the southern limits, the A4212 from Bala to Trawsfynydd providing the northern and the A470(T) from Dolgellau to Trawsfynydd forming the western.

Walk Summary: A very hard, long walk over some of the toughest mountains in Wales. This walk should not be underestimated. Although partly on paths and tracks, much of the route is over pathless terrain, some of it very wet and boggy, such as the crossing of the Migneint on Day One. This walk is only for those with experience of remote mountain areas, and with good navigational skills. Day One takes in the northern peaks of the range, traversing them anti-clockwise from Bala before bringing you down to the tiny bothy at Llyn Arenig Fawr for the night. Day Two takes you over Arenig Fawr, the highest mountain in the range. You then walk through the Coed y Brenin Forest to the delightful Penrhos-isaf bothy for the night. Day Three starts with an ascent of Rhobell Fawr before continuing on and over Dduallt before descending to Llanuwchllyn at the western end of Llyn Tegid (Lake Bala) where you catch the Bala Lake Railway back to the start point.

Transport:	Buses running between Dolgellau and Llangollen stop at Bala. The Bala Lake Railway will need to be used to take you from the end of your walk at Llanuwchllyn back to Bala. This only runs between April and September, so at other times of the year it is best to park at Llanuwchllyn and take a taxi to Bala to start your walk. Call the Bala Lake Railway Company for details of services (tel. 01678 540666).
Accommodation and supplies:	There are Loads of B&Bs in Bala, or try the Coach House self-catering bunkhouse at Tomen y Castell just outside the town to the east (tel. 01678 520738). There are not any good campsites in Bala, unless you want to pay for the extravagances of Pen-y-Bont near the Bala Lake Railway station. There is a small, basic but comfortable campsite north of Bala at Tynddol (grid ref. SH 912 385). There are shops and a couple of small supermarkets in Bala, including a small outdoor shop. There are no other supply points along the route.
Overnight Options:	This three-day route has been devised around the use of the bothies at Llyn Arenig Fawr and Penrhos-isaf. The former is a very small affair, basic, but with a fireplace and small sleeping platform. It can be found beneath the east wall of the dam at Llyn Arenig Fawr (grid ref. SH 850 378). Penrhos-isaf lies deep with the Coed y Brenin Forest. It is a much bigger building, with a few rooms to choose from (grid ref. SH 737 238).

Day One: The Northern Arenigs

Start by walking north along the B4391 into **Bala** from the railway station. Turn right at the junction with the A494(T). Cross the road and walk eastwards along this, behind a screen of saplings to a bend in the road. Here a public footpath heads

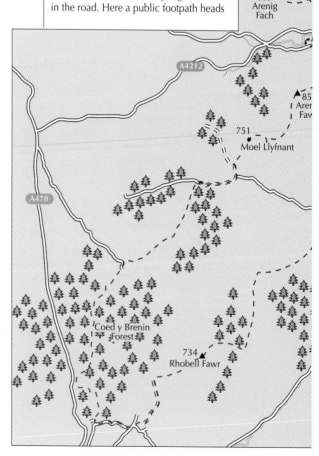

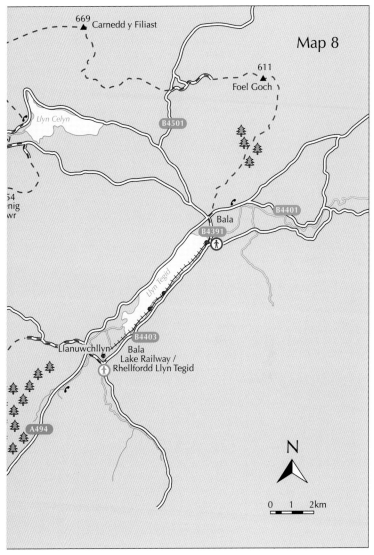

Map 8

669 Carnedd y Filiast

611 Foel Goch

Llyn Celyn

B4501

B4401

Bala

B4391

...54
...nig
...wr

Llyn Tegid

B4403

Llanuwchllyn

Bala Lake Railway / Rheilffordd Llyn Tegid

N

0   1   2km

The summit of Foel Goch, meaning 'red bare hill', is marked by a trig pillar, a cairn and a boundary marker. This is a great viewpoint for the Snowdon Range over the Moelwyns. Moel Siabod partly blocks the views of the Glyderau and Carneddau behind, but this is still one of the finest viewpoints in Snowdonia.

Carnedd y Filiast means 'cairn of the greyhound bitch', though we will never know where the hill got its name. All around on these heather-clad slopes you will hear red grouse cackling away at you as you walk. If you are really luck you may also get to see a short-eared owl that hunts during the day on these open moors.

north across pastures to climb up to a minor road. Turn left by a small house, then right after 100m and continue uphill to Y Gloig before heading east down to cross a stream. Climb up the other side and make for Tai-draw, leaving this farm behind by heading east uphill towards the forest edge. Enter the forest and walk north-east on a vague path around the southern flank of two little knolls to Maes-y-fedw. Re-enter the forest to the north-east and follow public footpaths through to Creigiau, crossing the stream there and heading out around the south-eastern flank of Gawr Fynydd to descend into the narrow valley of the Nant Cefn-coch. Cross the stream to Pentre-tai-yn-y-cwm where another small, narrow valley joins the main one, and pick up a public footpath up the eastern side of this gorge, formed by the Nant Cwm-da. Two ridges hem you in here, Moel Darren to the west and Orddu to the east. Continue up the valley to gain the ridge above at a col between Orddu and Foel Goch. Turn left along the ridge line to reach the summit of **Foel Goch** at 611m. ◄

Walking westwards along the ridge will help keep you on the high ground all the way to Garnedd Fawr, descend to Greigwen from there and picking up a public footpath out to the B4501 at Nant-gau. Turn left for a short way down the road, then right off the road and onto a public footpath that leads across fields to Nant Hir. An alarming number of paths and tracks seem to radiate from Nant Hir, and you should take the main track heading north-west up the broad ridge to the farm at Bwlch Graianog, from where the ridge of Graig Ddu is reached. Descend westwards into the lovely valley of Cwm Hesgyn and pick up a good landrover track climbing up the opposite side to Ffridd Cwmhesgyn. This leads just north of west up towards the minor summit of Foel-boeth, but just before that top a junction in the track on the right should be taken to cross the chattering stream of the Nant y Coed before climbing onwards to the summit of **Carnedd y Filiast** at 669m. ◄

Now follows one of the toughest parts of this tough walk – the crossing of the eastern Migneint. Fortunately, navigation is not a problem here as you will have a fence to follow all the way to the northern slopes of Arenig Fach. Simply walk westwards along the southern side of the fence, passing the little rise of Carnedd Llechwedd-llyfn on your left. This is all very boggy ground, but none more so than around the Afon Gelyn which you must cross to gain the heathery slopes of Arenig Fach ahead. Do not be tempted to make directly for Arenig Fach however, as that way lies much difficult ground. It is far easier to continue along the side of the fence to a point north-west of **Arenig Fach's** summit, from where an old line of fence posts leads up to the rim of the small summit plateau. The summit itself lies just above and is marked by a large cairn and trig pillar. ▸

Getting off Arenig Fach can be a problem. There are paths, but none of them are obvious. However, the best route seems to be to head east down the broad ridge of Bryn Du, which has a vague path running along a line of fence posts down to the main road running around the western shores of Llyn Celyn Reservoir.

Walk westwards along the A4212 for a short way until you see a public footpath on the left leading down to a bridge over the Afon Tryweryn. Continue around the western side of a knoll to cross an old railway line where you gain a minor lane. Turn left along this for 1km to a track on the right. Follow this up and over a little moor to Llyn Arenig Fawr. The bothy lies at the eastern-most point of the lake and you should spend the night here.

Day Two: Arenig Fawr and the Coed-y-Brenin Forest

From the bothy, start the day by crossing the dam on a good path and climbing up the superb ridge of Y Castell to a flat area above the crags that give the ridge its name. Head west for the main ridge of Arenig Fawr where you will meet an old line of fence posts. A well-worn path runs along this line and you should turn left and follow it to the summit of **Arenig Fawr** where a trig pillar is built into the huge cairn shelter. ▸

Llyn Celyn, or 'holly lake', was dammed in 1965, amongst much controversy, to provide water for Liverpool. The village of Capel Celyn was lost beneath the waters and is today commemorated by a memorial chapel nearby.

There is a memorial within the summit cairn shelter to Canadian airmen who died here when their plane crashed during the Second World War.

Walk south from the summit, down into a little narrow col. Climb the other side to a subsidiary summit, then take a bearing south-westwards for a col between this mountain mass and that of Moel Llyfnant, your next objective over to the south-west. The going is at first stony but leads down to easy grass slopes then on to the col itself, which can be boggy at times.

The climb up **Moel Llyfnant** from the col is very steep and direct. Simply head westwards up the eastern flank of the mountains and you will soon find yourself standing on the obvious summit knoll at 750m above sea level. This is another very fine viewpoint.

Descend to the south-west, aiming for the track that runs along the eastern side of Afon Lliw in the valley to the west. Turn left along the track and walk out to the minor 'Mountain Road' at Blaen-Lliw. Turn right along the Mountain Road, crossing the Afon Lliw then climbing to a ridge beside a forestry plantation. Continue to the top of the hill at the 531m spot height, then leave the road on the left and follow the top edge of the forest to the minor peak of Moel y Feidiog. From here much

Descending
Arenig Fawr

rough ground leads you along the vague ridge heading south-west for the little peak of Bryn-pig. South-west again there is a sharp loop in another narrow road at a place called Tai-cynhauaf (unnamed on the Landranger maps, but marked by a cattle grid). Head down to this loop in the road, then walk west along the road for 700m to a public footpath on the left leading downhill to Bryn-y-gath. Follow the footpath down to the south-west, contouring at first to the little farmstead at Bedd-y-coedwr, from where the footpath leads down beside the forest edge to the gushing Afon Mawddach. Follow this downstream for 1km to a bridge that takes you over to the east side of the river by the spectacular falls of the Rhaeadr Mawddach. Walk southwards along this good track all the way to the car park and bridge leading over the river to Ganllwyd. Do not cross the bridge but look for a public footpath on the left climbing very steeply up through the trees to the ridge top, deep in the forest. Here you will join a forest track and should turn southwards, bearing first right then left at the junctions you will come to. Soon after the left-hand turn at the second junction you will come to a little track on the right leaving the main track. This leads directly to Penrhos-isaf bothy. There is a stream up and behind the bothy that you can get water from at a little tank.

Day Three: Rhobell Fawr and Dduallt

Leave the bothy by heading out onto the main track by which you came in last night, then turn right and follow it downhill for almost 1km, turning left at a junction and walking on downhill to a minor road. Turn right along the road to a bridge over the Afon Wen, then left at another junction and climb steeply uphill still on the road until you come to a crossroads. Go straight ahead to Llanfachreth village. Head eastwards through the village, looking for the village school just beyond a right bend. Continue along the road beyond the bend, around a sharp left, then a sharp right to a track heading uphill on the left to Cors-y-garnedd. Take this gated road up through the farms until it becomes a track leading over the south-west ridge of Rhobell Fawr at Bwlch Goriwared. Leave the track here and climb up the narrowing south-west ridge to the summit of **Rhobell Fawr** at 784m. There is a big cairn marking the highest point.

To continue, head north for 100m or so to pick up an old stone wall and fence, climbing over this via a stile then heading downhill to the right alongside it. This leads to a broad track among the trees of a forestry plantation. Head north to a newly cleared area on the right, then walk along the northern boundary of this heading east to the other side of what was once the planted area. This leads to a boggy, flat expanse on the south ridge of Dduallt and you should pick a way along the rough slopes to the east of the forest to the rocky little top of Dduallt at 657 metres just beside a fence.

Return to the fence and follow it northwards down in a series of rocky steps interspersed with very boggy ground to the head of the Afon Mawddach. Cross the river, at times difficult after heavy rain, then follow vague paths marked on the maps as a public footpath, eastwards through the shallow valley that lies between the ridges of Cerrig yr Iwrch to the south and Cerrig Chwibanog to the north. The path becomes a bit more distinct at an angle in the fence, then becomes a track as it heads into the Coed Bryn Bras Forest. Follow the track downhill to another track that contours the hillside here. Turn right and cross the Afon Fwy via a footbridge. Walk eastwards along the track until it joins a narrow public road. Bear right here, still heading east to the farms at Deildre and out to the busy A494(T) at Pen-y-bont. Turn right along the road and veer left at the big junction in **Llanuwchllyn** to reach the car park and station on the Bala Lake Railway where this fantastic walk ends.

9 – The Main Ridge of the Arans

Total Distance:	42km
Daily Distances:	1) 19km 2) 17km
Maps:	OS Landranger, sheet 124 *Dolgellau and Porthmadog*
Starting Point:	There is a little car park just under the bridge on the west side of the Afon Twrch in Llanuwchllyn village, at the western end of Llyn Tegid (Lake Bala). Grid ref. SH 879 297

Area Summary: The Arans form what is possibly one of the finest and longest single ridges in Wales, reaching a height of 907m on Aran Fawddwy itself. They are also one of the main mountain masses of the Principality, although not often recognised as such. The range is parallel to the busy A494 which runs along its western base. To the east the boundaries of the range is less well defined, as the vast moorlands of the Arans merge with those of the Hirnants, but are separated from them by a minor road from Dinas Mawddwy to Llanuwchllyn at the Bwlch y Groes.

Walk Summary: A relatively easy and short walk over generally good ground with paths to follow throughout on Day One, although on Day Two you will be walking over pathless and often very boggy terrain. The walk on Day One follows the crest of this fantastic ridge all the way from Llanuwchllyn in the north through to the most southerly summit of the group, Pen y Brynfforchog, before finding a wild campsite high on the ridge of Y Gribin. Day Two begins with a steep descent into the fine mountain valley of Cwm Cywarch from where you cross over into the little visited territory to the east of the main ridge.

Transport:	Buses running between Dolgellau and Llangollen stop at Llanuwchllyn. The Bala Lake Railway can also be used between April and September to reach Llanuwchllyn from Bala. Call the Bala Lake Railway Company for details of services (tel. 01678 540666).
Accommodation and supplies:	Loads of B&Bs in Bala at the far end of the lake from Llanuwchllyn, or try the Coach House self-catering bunkhouse at Tomen y Castell just outside the town to the east (tel. 01678 520738). There are not any good campsites in Bala, unless you want to pay for the extravagances of Pen-y-Bont near the Bala Lake Railway station. There is a small, basic but comfortable campsite north of Bala at Tynddol (grid ref. SH 912 385). Going the other way there is a great guesthouse in Dolgellau up on the Cadair Idris road called Bryn yr Odyn (tel. 01341 423470). There are shops and a couple of small supermarkets in both Bala and Dolgellau, including small outdoor shops. There are no other supply points along the route.
Overnight Options:	You should aim to camp wild on the small col to the north-west of Y Gribin (grid ref. SH 842 179), or it is possible to descend to Dinas Mawddwy to the south-east and camp at the site there or use one of the B&Bs that have sprung up there along the route of the Cambrian Way.

Day One: The Main Ridge of the Arans

Directly opposite the car park by the south-western corner of the bridge over the Afon Twrch in **Llanuwchllyn**, a public footpath leaves the road and starts to climb, gently at first, up the long, northern ridge of the Arans towards distant Aran Benllyn. Take this route, bearing right at the first junction where the main track goes straight ahead, then left at another point just below a little knoll to the left after 1km. The ridge is very easy to follow as it soon narrows perceptibly, though the first summit, Aran Benllyn, is a long time coming. As you climb, the deep valley of Cwm Croes forms a verdant trench to the left while the heavily forested slopes of the Aton Dyfrdwy mark the flanks of the ridge to the right.

Six kilometres from Llanuwchllyn you pass by a small tarn, then over a ruined stone wall and find yourself on the summit of **Aran Benllyn** at 884m.

Erw y Ddafad-ddu

> Aran Benllyn means 'mountain at the head of the lake', although it is often said that this refers to the hollow containing Llyn Lliwbran beneath the mountain's north-east slopes rather than the tiny Llyn Pen Aran passed by on the ascent. Many feel now though that the name is a simple reference to Llyn Tegid, or Bala Lake itself at the head of which Aran Benllyn rises.

Llyn Lliwbran on the eastern side of the ridge as you ascended has gained notoriety for its botanical interest in the past. It was visited on April 17th 1682 by the youthful plant-hunter Edward Lhuyd. He thoroughly searched the entire area of the cirque in which the lake rests, including 'ye rivulets that run through ye rocks above Llyn Llymbran'. This unusual spelling of the name is

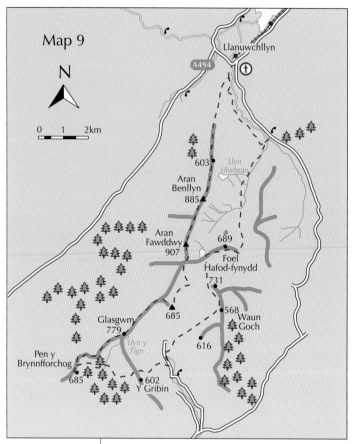

Map 9

N

0   1   2km

Llanuwchllyn

A494

603

*Llyn
Lliwbran*

Aran
Benllyn
885

Aran
Fawddwy
907

689

Foel
Hafod-fynydd
731

568
Waun
Goch

685

Glasgwm
779

*Llyn y
Fign*

616

Pen y
Brynnfforchog
685

602
Y Gribin

pretty much the same as the current pronunciation of the word by the locals today. The late William Condry in his Collins New Naturalist book, *The Snowdonia National Park*, notes that this suggests a corruption of 'Llyn Bran' which probably means the lake of the crow, but also points out that Bran is an old name connected with very early Celtic folklore. He notes that some authorities do insist on using Llymbren.

Leave the summit of Aran Benllyn and walk just west of south down to the col that separates this summit from the next, Erw y Ddafad-ddu. Climb easily up to the flat top of this hill with a small cairn overlooking the head of Cwm Llwydd at 872m. ▸

Another kilometre to the south lies the rocky top of **Aran Fawddwy** at 907m. This is the high point of the Arans range and provides a fine viewpoint. It is an easy walk alongside a fence to just west of the summit from where an obvious path leads up to the top.

Aran Fawddwy, meaning simply 'the mountain of (Dinas) Mawddwy', is the highest mountain in Britain south of Snowdon itself. The translation of the name Mawddwy can also be worked out; in Walter Parry Haskett Smith's book of *Climbing in the British Isles* he tells us that 'The word Aran means and "alp", or a "high place"; mawdd is said to mean "spreading", and the terminations ach or wy mean "water".' We are therefore left with 'the high place of the spreading water' – very apt for Aran Fawddwy. Creiglyn Dyfi lies right underneath the east face of the summit, and this is the source of the mighty River Dovey.

Head south from the summit of Aran Fawddwy, ignoring the main path which goes off to the south-west. Skirt around the cliffs to your left until this narrows to a grassy ridge. Here you will find a memorial and visitor's book in a small tin box beneath a cairn. ▸

Do not continue along the narrowing ridge from here, but instead head south-west around the rim of the cwm, keeping the gaping drop to your left. This takes you down to a grassy col with a rocky knoll at its heart. From here you should climb up to the south to the fine summit of Gwaun y Llwyni at 685m. ▸

Head south-west from the summit of Gwaun y Llwyni, going down the ridge to the rim of the cliffs of

Erw y Ddafad-ddu means simply 'acre of the black sheep', presumably referring to the acre of flat ground at the summit.

The cairn commemorates the death of Mike Aspain, a member of the RAF St Athan Mountain Rescue Team. Mike died here after being struck by lightning whilst out on duty with the other teams members. He was only 18 years old.

Views from Gwaun y Llwyni, or moorland of the bushes, are fantastic, taking in the deep trench of Hengwm to the east.

Aran Fawddwy

Glasgwm, meaning 'blue valley', rises to 779m and has right by the summit cairn a large tarn, Llyn y Fign.

Creigiau Camddwr, then handrailing around these to the west and across to a broad and very boggy col to the north of Glasgwm. Here you'll pick up a path leading up the north-east face of **Glasgwm** to its lovely summit. ◄

Leave the summit of Glasgwm by heading south-west down a broad ridge. This soon brings you to the top corner of a forest, from where you should head west along the outside of the trees to Bwlch y Fign. Climb west to a little sausage-shaped summit, then south alongside the forest still to the summit of **Pen y Brynfforchog**.

Pen y Brynfforchog means 'top of the forked hill', and lies at 685m above sea level. The summit lies atop the westernmost of two little knolls and is marked by a small cairn.

Head back north from the summit to the edge of the forest again, then at a point 300m from the summit a track heads off into the forest to the right. Follow this eastwards above a small stream. Continue eastwards for 1km, crossing a small stream where it may be wise to fill your water bottles for a night out. Cross the stream and continue east, then south-eastwards until you come to a much bigger track leading out of the forest. Follow this to a little col to the north-west of **Y Gribin** and camp here for the night.

Day Two: Hengwm and Cwm Croes

Start the day by heading down to the north-east from your lofty campsite. A public footpath leads the way in tight zigzags from the col immediately west of Y Gribin and you should soon find yourself descending through slatey scree into the beautiful valley of Cwm Cywarch. The path takes you down to the minor road that leads up this quiet corner of the National Park and you should turn left along this to the farmstead at Blaencywarch. From this point a footpath heads off into the mountains to the north-east, taking you high above the valley of Hengwm and along the slopes of Pen yr Allt Uchaf (unnamed on the Landranger map). The path climbs gradually to a broad grassy and sometimes boggy col at 568m, and here turns to the north up the wide ridge of Drysgol. Climb up to this minor summit, hop over the fence by the ridge and descend through rough ground to the head of Llaethnant. The going is boggy and takes you through much heather, tussock grass and hard rushes, but the stream of Llaethnant is soon reached.

From the stream climb to the north to the outflow of the superb setting of Creiglyn Dyfi, the source of the Afon Dyfi (River Dovey), then walk around to its northern most point. The main Aran ridge fills the view to the west, and the dark crags of Aran Fawddwy itself thrust from out of the lake. What appears to be a small knoll lies to the east of the lake and you should climb this to continue. Once on the top, it becomes clear that this is in fact a short ridge, leading over a minor summit known as **Foel Hafod-fynydd** (again unnamed on the Landranger map). Walk along the ridge to the east, keeping on the southern side of a fence that runs along it. After a couple of hundred metres another fence heads off to the north, down steep slopes to the col at Bwlch Sirddyn. Climb

The east face of Aran Fawddwy from the ridge of Foel Hafod-Fynydd

over the ridge fence and follow this new one down to the col. Here a public footpath crosses the range and you should turn left, dropping into the valley of Cwm Croes, known as Cwm Ddu here at its head. The path keeps to the right hand side of a stream as you descend, then crosses it down in the valley bottom. From here a good track heads off down the cwm along its western side, and you should follow this down the valley to the farms at Talardd. A public footpath turns off to the north-west and leads through fields back to the main track just above **Llanuwchllyn**. Turn right along this track and follow it back into the village and the end of a great walk.

10 – Around the Source
of the River Dovey

Total Distance:	46km
Daily Distances:	1) 24km 2) 22km
Maps:	OS Landranger, sheet 124 *Dolgellau and Porthmadog*
Starting Point:	There is a little car park just under the bridge on the west side of the Afon Twrch in Llanuwchllyn village at the western end of Llyn Tegid (Lake Bala). Grid ref. SH 879 297
Finishing Point:	The main square in Dolgellau, grid ref. SH 728 177

Area Summary: The Arans form what is possibly one of the finest and longest single ridges in Wales, reaching a height of 907m on Aran Fawddwy itself. They are also one of the main mountain masses of the Principality, although not often recognised as such. The range is parallel to the busy A494 which runs along its western base. To the east the boundaries of the range is less well defined, as the vast moorlands of the Arans merge with those of the Hirnants, but are separated from them by a minor road from Dinas Mawddwy to Llanuwchllyn at the Bwlch y Groes. The Dovey Hills rise to the south of the Arans, beyond the Ochr y Bwlch taken by the A470. This range is much ignored by hillwalkers, which is a great shame as the ridge walking here is fantastic. Forested slopes cover the southern approaches to these hills, while very steep faces edges by sharp ridges rise to the flat, moorland tops.

Walk Summary: A fairly strenuous walk over generally good ground with paths to follow for the most part. On

Transport: Buses running between Dolgellau and Llangollen stop at Llanuwchllyn. Best to leave the car at Llanuwchllyn, then catch a bus back from Dolgellau.

Accommodation and supplies: There are loads of B&Bs in Bala at the far end of the lake from Llanuwchllyn, or try the Coach House self-catering bunkhouse at Tomen y Castell just outside the town to the east (tel. 01678 520738). Going the other way, there is a great guesthouse in Dolgellau up on the Cadair Idris road called Bryn yr Odyn (tel. 01341 423470). There are shops and a couple of small supermarkets in both Bala and Dolgellau, including small outdoor shops. There is a small shop in Dinas Mawddwy.

Overnight Options: You should aim to camp at the official site in Dinas Mawddwy (grid ref. SH 859 152), or use one of the B&Bs that have sprung up there along the route of the Cambrian Way.

both days you may be walking over often boggy terrain. The walk on Day One follows the deep valley of Cwm Croes from Llanuwchllyn in the north through to a high pass at Bwlch Sirddyn from where you head

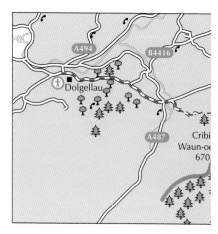

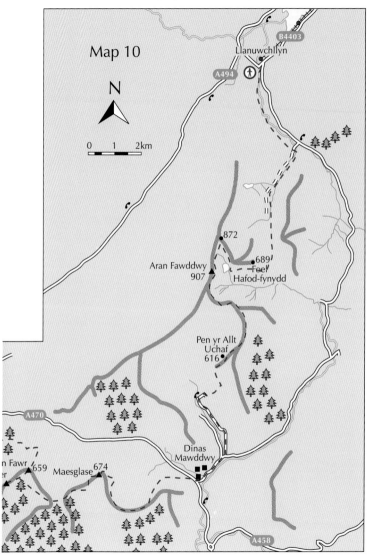

over an intervening bump to Creiglyn Dyfi, the source of the Afon Dyfi (River Dovey). From here you gain the main Aran ridge and follow it southwards to a camp or B&B at Dinas Mawddwy. Day Two begins with a steep ascent onto the Dovey Hills, and then takes a route over the three summits of this range before descending to Dolgellau.

Day One: To the Source of the Afon Dyfi

Directly opposite the car park by the south-western corner of the bridge over the Afon Twrch in **Llanuwchllyn**, a public footpath leaves the road and starts to climb, gently at first, up towards the long, northern ridge of the Arans and distant Aran Benllyn. At the first junction, where the main track to the summits heads off to the right, continue southwards, taking the route to the left high above the gushing waters of the Afon Twrch. This leads to Plas-Morgan where it becomes a public footpath. Follow this alongside but above the river to Talardd at the foot of Cwm Croes and descend into the cwm to a track that leads up its length. Turn right here and follow the track

Creiglyn Dyfi

up the western bank of the river, up into the head of
Cwm Croes. Here the track leads to a crossing of the
stream where two cirques lie above, Cwm Llwydd to the
right and Cwm Ddu to the left. A public footpath climbs
up into Cwm Ddu, along the eastern side of the stream
issuing from it, and you should follow this southwards
up to a boggy col known as Bwlch Sirddyn. The footpath continues over the other side of the bwlch, but you
should leave it here and take to the steep hillside to the
right. A fence leads upwards to a ridgeline above and
here you should hop over another fence and turn right
along the ridge to the summit of **Foel Hafod-fynydd**, a
minor summit.

Follow the ridge westwards then down to a vague
col to your first view of the source of the Afon Dyfi, the
beautiful mountain tarn of Creiglyn Dyfi backed by the
imposing ramparts of Aran Fawddwy.

William Condry, in his Collins New Naturalist book,
The Snowdonia National Park, writes of this cwm
that, 'There are good mountain plants such as the
green spleenwort, and that rather choosy calcicole
always gives the botanist hope of other good things.
Then there are ravens and ring ouzels, kestrels and
buzzards. And it was on the slopes round the Dovey
lake that George Bolam, while botanising on the
cliffs above, saw a pine-marten and watched it hunting for half an hour. He also found "a very good flint
arrowhead" in a near-by stream-bed, good evidence
that man had affairs to attend to in those remote cor-
ries maybe three or four thousand years ago.'

From Creiglyn Dyfi a steep grassy bank with occasional eroded steps leads up to the north-west to the flat
summit of Erw y Ddafad-ddu, which translates literally
as 'acre of the black sheep'. Here a small cairn marks the
highest point at 872m.

*Aran Fawddwy and Creiglyn Dyfi –
the source of the River Dovey*

Now you are on the main ridge of the Arans and should turn southwards along a well-used track to the rocky little summit of **Aran Fawddwy**, the highest summit of the Arans at 907m, and Britain's tallest mountain south of Snowdon itself. ▸

Leave the summit and head south, ignoring the track that goes off towards the south-west. Your path curves around to the little summit of Drws Bach, and then turns east to the top of Drysgol. Continue along the main track as it bends to the south-east down to a col at 568m, from where you should ignore the main track heading down into Hengwm, but continue instead up the moorland ridge to the south, curving around to the little summit of **Pen yr Allt Uchaf**. At 620m this minor top fails to live up to its grand name. It translates as 'top of the highest hillside'.

Continuing along a narrowing ridge to the south-west, you can descend for 1km to spot height 545m, then take the steep grassy slopes down into Cwm Terwyn to the south-east. Here you will meet a public footpath that leads down into the main valley, Cwm Cywarch at Ty'n-y-maes. Walk down the driveway of the farm to a little chapel, then turn left and walk down the valley along the minor road to Aber-Cywarch and a T-junction. Here turn right and follow the lane into **Dinas Mawddwy** where you will find a bed for the night.

Day Two: Over the Dovey Hills to Dolgellau

From the centre of Dinas Mawddwy walk along the minor road to the west and out onto the main road, the A470(T) that bypasses the village. Turn right for a short way and cross over to a public footpath sign. Follow this steeply uphill through coniferous woodland to the slopes of Ffridd Gulcwm and around to the head of a large, steeply angled cwm. Here broken rocks form the head of the cwm and your route takes you around the left-hand side of these, following the ridge up and handrailing along to the summit of **Maesglase** at 674m. The summit is a broad expanse of open heather moorland, although

According to Walter Parry Haskett Smith in his book *Climbing in the British Isles* he tells us that 'The word Aran means and "alp", or a "high place"; mawdd is said to mean "spreading", and the terminations ach or wy mean "water".' We are therefore left with the translation 'high place of the spreading water' – very apt for Aran Fawddwy.

a path picks a way through this to the south-west and down to a narrow col below the little dome of Craig Portas. Follow the obvious path up and over this little knoll, then down into another col. Yet another knoll rises ahead to the west and you should climb over this and continue along the ridge as it turns to the north-west. At the next col you will see forested slopes down to the left, and here a track cuts across the hillside along the contour lines. Drop down to this track and follow it north-westwards around the head of the cwm until just under the col to the north-east of Waun-oer. Climb up to the col over rough ground, and then bear left up a nice little ridge to the summit of **Waun-oer**. An OS trig pillar and solar panel mark the highest point of Waun-oer at 670m. The name Waun-oer translates as 'the cold moor'.

Head back north-east from the summit along the ridge you have just taken. Drop back down to the col then climb up the south-west ridge of **Cribin Fawr**, a featureless plateau of grass and heather. ◄

The summit of Cribin Fawr is hard to find among the little tufts of grass on this flat top. There is no cairn or marker. The name translates as 'big serrated ridge'.

Walk north from the broad summit plateau down towards a narrowing ridge and follow this a short way down to a track that crosses over from the east to the west. Turn left and walk westwards into a very broad bowl. The track leads on to Gwanas-fawr and you should walk out along their driveway to the busy A470(T). Turn left along this busy road to the Cross Foxes Hotel, turning left at the junction then immediately right along a narrow lane. Follow this lane all the way to **Dolgellau** and the end of this walk.

11 – Cadair Idris and the Tarrens

Total Distance:	52km
Daily Distances:	1) 25km 2) 27km
Maps:	OS Landranger, sheets 124 *Dolgellau and Porthmadog* and 135 *Aberystwyth*
Starting Point:	Llanllwyda has a good campsite where you can stay overnight and leave your car during this backpack. Llanllwyda lies in the Dyffryn Dysynni, 2km up the valley from the famous Bird Rock, or Craig yr Aderyn (grid ref. SH 650 076)

Area Summary: Two very different ranges are crossed on this backpack. Cadair Idris is a well-known, rocky range rising to superb summits arranged around dramatic cwms. To the north of the range lies Dolgellau and the Mawddach Estuary, while to the south the quieter Afon Dysynni lies within a major geological trench cutting Cadair off from the Tarren range. The Tarrens are much gentler hills, and

Transport: There is no public transport to the start of this route.

Accommodation and supplies: There are plenty of accommodation options in Tywyn just down the valley from the start of this walk. Try the Ivy Guest House near the tourist office (tel 01654 711058). Alternatively, you can camp at Llanllwyda itself, which is a fine site deep in the mountains (tel 01654 782276). There are plenty of shops in Tywyn, and some supplies are available during the walk at Corris.

Overnight Options: Either stay in the youth hostel in Corris (tel. 01654 761686), (grid ref. SH 753 081) or try the Briach Goch Hotel (tel. 01654 761229)

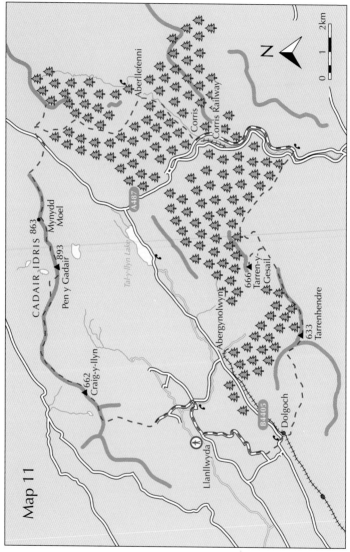

Map 11

Aberllefenni

Corris

Corris Railway

N

2km
1
0

A487

CADAIR IDRIS 863

Mynydd Moel

893
Pen y Gadair

Tal-y-llyn Lake

Tarren-y-Gesail
666

Tarrenhendre
633

Abergynolwyn

662
Craig-y-llyn

Dolgoch

B4405

Llanllwyda

are cloaked in forestry. This makes for a very varied walking experience. The superb lower reaches of the River Dovey define the southern extremes of the Tarrens.

Walk Summary: A truly fantastic route offering a wide variety of terrain. Paths on Cadair Idris are usually very well signposted and hence eroded, but this route takes you via little-walked valleys and ridges to the summits before crossing over the valley to the east into the southern half of the Dovey Hills and deep into the forests around Corris. Day Two then climbs onto the wide flanks of the Tarrens before descending into the cleft of the Dyffryn Dysynni. The walk then takes you over quiet hills back to the start at Llanllwyda.

Day One: The Cadair Idris Range from the Dyffryn Dysynni

For such a well-trodden range of hills, this route onto the Cadair Idris massif takes you through some remarkably quiet countryside. The start of the walk itself is far from obvious. Leave the campsite at **Llanllwyda** along the road and head north-east up the valley. Turn left over the bridge, the Pont Ystumanner, and then left again at the next junction. This lane leads north-west to Nant Caw where a public footpath climbs up the east side of the valley above. Here the route is not easy to follow, although higher up a series of stiles gives the game away and will put you on the right track, bringing you out onto open moorland below the spot height 583m at the south-western end of the fine ridge of **Craig-y-lynn**. Bash up through the rough ground to gain the ridge and walk along it to the summit at 622m.

Continue along the ridge to the north-east, dropping down to a col then up the other side along a good path to the fine summit of Tyrrau Mawr. All along this part of the route broken crags of shale falls away to the north-west. Tyrrau Mawr translates as 'high towers', although the summit itself is only 661m above sea level. Rough grass and bilberry clothe the slopes all around its top.

Cadair Idris from
Barmouth

From the summit of Tyrrau Mawr the path turns east and descends easily by some large cairns to an eroded pass. This is the place where the Pony Path crosses the range from the Mawddach (to the north) to the Dyffryn Dysynni (to the south) and also gives one of the most popular and the easiest walkers route to the summit of Cadair Idris itself.

Follow the Pony Path up to the east for a few hundred yards, then turn away as it makes for the south-east and a high col that stands between Cyfrwy and the summit of Cadair itself, known as **Pen y Gadair**. Ignore the path to the col and instead head east on a bearing to the fine rocky top of Cyfrwy.

From the summit of Cyfrwy, walk south-east along the rim of the cliff-line that falls away dramatically to the north. You will soon find yourself at the col at which the Pony Path gains the high tops. Continue handrailing along the top of the crags, turning to the east as rocky ground rises and takes you to the highest point of the Cadair Idris range, **Pen y Gadair** at 893m.

A trig pillar marks the highest point of this fine mountain, while there is a little mountain hut which can be used for shelter a fewm away to the north. Richard Pugh of Dolgellau, one of the earliest guides on Cadair Idris, built the hut in the 1830s. It was said that this hut 'proved of great advantage to visitors who before were not unfrequently assailed by the teeming shower without an opportunity of shelter; and who had no spot for temporary refreshment while waiting for the dispersion of the misty clouds in order to enjoy the exquisite prospect. Here parties and individuals may have all convenient refreshment.'

The name Cadair Idris means the 'chair of Idris' and this is generally taken to refer to the high cirque which holds Lynn y Gadair beneath the summit slopes to the north. Others make mention of a rock near the summit; if you spend the night upon it you will wake either a poet or a lunatic!

Cadair Idris
from Dyssyni

Leave the summit of Pen y Gadair along a stony track heading north-east, then east across an open plateau to the distant rocks adorning the summit of **Mynydd Moel**. This can be reached by handrailing along the rim of the cliffs which still fall away in long broken faces to the north. The summit lies just beyond a fence and stile.

Now turn south-east and follow the path down steeply to a ridge running out to the fine little rocky top of Gau Graig. ◄

Great views open out from Gau Graig, taking in the length of the huge geological fault that stretches along the south side of Cadair Idris and holds Tal-y-llyn as well as Lake Bala right over in the far north-east.

Turn south from Gau Graig and pick up a narrow path that drops steeply towards the main road (the A487(T)) at the top of the pass. This path is obvious but care must be taken as it is very steep and winds its way around one or two rocky crags.

Once on the main road turn left along it for a couple of 100m to where a public footpath sign points up the hillside on the opposite side. Take this up through steep, heather-covered ground to a path junction which climbs up a little cwm. Turn right and follow this second path uphill and over the shoulder of Mynydd Fron-fraith. On the shoulder you will see a forestry plantation

Tal-y-llyn

ahead and you should follow the eastern side of this down into the valley at Waenllefenni. Walk down the track to join the minor road at its end, but do not walk along it. Instead a delightful path turns off to the right and follows a parallel line through the farms of Fronfraith and Hen-gae before turning south-east towards the village of **Aberllefenni**. Once in the village turn right along the narrow lane and follow it for 3km into the bigger village of **Corris** where you should find a bed for the night.

Day Two: Along the Ridge of the Tarrens

Start the day by walking south through Corris village on the minor road that runs along the eastern side of the valley. This is a quiet lane and is a delight to follow right through to the Centre for Alternative Technology (CAT).

Just before the CAT a lane leads off to the right to cross the bridge near Llwyngwern campsite and you should take this road out to the main road at Pantperthog. Turn left along the main road until you come to a chapel on the right after 200m. A forest track on the right follows the north bank of the Nant y Darren and leads into the high eastern corrie of Tarren y Geseil where the trees thin out. Walk south to a little disused quarry, then around to the corner of the forest to the south-east of the summit of **Tarren y Geseil**. Here a vague path takes you up the edge of the forest to the ridge, and you can turn left along this to reach the summit at 666m.

> It is better to avoid using the term 'Tarren Hills' as is common among hillwalkers, as 'Tarren' itself means 'hill' or 'knoll'. Tarren y Geseil translates as 'knoll of the hollow'. An OS trig pillar marks the summit.

Return along the fence to the corner of the forest to the south-east of the summit, then pick up a vague path leading directly into the thick of the trees. This soon opens out a little, and takes you more easily to the intervening top of Foel y Geifr. Drop down off the south-west ridge of this little hill to pick up a track that will lead you all the way up the long eastern ridge of **Tarrenhendre**. ◄

Tarrenhendre translates as 'knoll of the winter dwelling' and is a fine viewpoint among much peaty heather.

Head north-west from the summit to pick up a good track that leads down into the cwm of the Nant Dolgoch. Continue along the track for a short way until a path crosses the stream in a fine oak woodland and takes you down to the railway at **Dolgoch** below the superb Dolgoch Falls. Walk out to the B4405 road and turn left. At a sharp bend left, after just 200m, a public footpath leads off to the right and you should follow this north-westwards to the farm at Tŷ -mawr. Turn right along the track here and follow it through some fine, knolly country to the farm at Bwlch-y-maen. Just beyond this farm a public footpath to the left leads directly down to **Llanllwyda** and the end of a great two-days' walk.

12 – Exploring the Ridges around the Tanat Valley

Total Distance:	53km
Daily Distances:	1) 30km 2) 23km
Maps:	OS Landranger, sheet 125 *Bala and Lake Vyrnwy*, *Berwyn*
Starting Point:	The charming little village of Llanrhaeadr-ym-Mochnant is a great place from which to walk. Start here in the village square (grid ref. SJ 124 261).

Area Summary: The western Berwyns, or Hirnants as they are invariably known nowadays, are among the hardest hills to walk in Wales. Here we scratch the surface by taking a long approach up to one of the remotest summits in the entire group, Cyrniau Nod. The Tanat valley cuts deep into the range and has the B4391 running along its length and over the hills themselves towards Bala.

Walk Summary: A surprisingly difficult walk over very tough ground. The going is mainly through thigh-deep heather throughout, much of it pathless, other than a few

Transport: There is no public transport to the start of this route.

Accommodation and supplies: There are good B&Bs in Llanrhaeadr-ym-Mochnant. Try Rose Cottage (tel 01691 780398) or Plas-y-Llan (tel 01691 780236). There are shops here, from which you can buy limited supplies, and also a couple of good pubs.

Overnight Options: Try the Bryntirion Inn (tel 01678 530205) just outside Llandderfel, or camp at Bryn Melyn just down the road to the east.

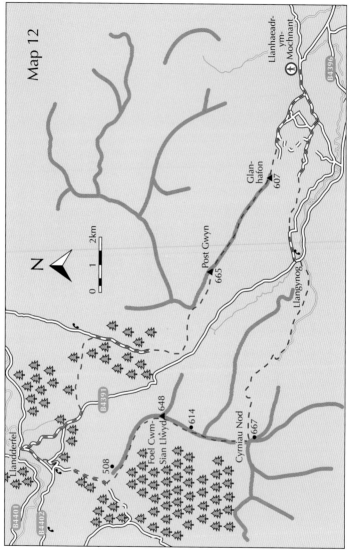

Map 12

Llanhaeadr-
ym-
Mochnant

B4396

Glan-
hafon
▲607

Post Gwyn
▲665

N

0   1   2km

Llangynog

B4391

Foel Cwm-
Sian Llwyd ▲648

614

Cyrniau Nod
▲667

Llandderfel

508

B4401

B4402

sections of road walking along quiet lanes. Although over moorland rather than mountain terrain, this is not a walk to be underestimated. I personally think it is possibly the toughest walk in this book, but then I have had a long association with these hills and have time and time again vowed never to go back. You have been warned! That said, I do keep going back, for here you'll find a solitude and beauty not easily witnessed elsewhere in Wales, and for those seeking a challenge of a different kind, there's no better place. The route leaves the lonely valley of the River Tanat and makes a gentle way onto the hills to the west, turning north from Cyrniau Nod towards the River Dee. Day Two is slightly easier and more often trod, taking you over the summit of Post Gwyn and back into the Tanat after yet more deep heather.

Day One: The Wilds of the Hirnants

Start the walk by heading west from **Llanrhaeadr-ym-Mochnant** on the road to Penybontfawr. This takes you up past the chapel and climbs gently for just over 2km to the farm at Plas-Du. A lane opposite the farm should then be taken heading north-west to another little chapel on the left. Just beyond this point take the next left at the junction and follow the lane through to Mochnant. Continue along this heading north-westwards to a public footpath that leads through a delightful wood, over a stream and on to the farm at Llwyn Onn. The path goes on the uphill side of the farm, passing beneath another fine deciduous wood, then via the farm at Ochr-glan-hafon to a narrow lane at Tai-uchaf. Turn right along the lane and walk down this into the little village of **Llangynog**.

Throughout this part of the walk you have been keeping to north bank of the Afon Tanat, a fine river where you can see dippers, grey wagtails and even the illusive otter. Buzzards can be seen circling above while peregrine falcon may be nesting on the crags above on Craig Rhiwarth.

Otter in the Tanat
Valley

Turn left into the village, cross the bridge and take the next left into Cwm Pennant. This is a superb valley, thought by many to be one of the most scenic in the whole of Wales.

Walk along the narrow lane right up into the head of the valley, passing the small community of Pennant Melangell and continuing to the road end where a public bridleway leads up on the right. Take this for 200m, looking for a track on the left that you should follow north-westwards up the side of the hill to a point above the fine waterfalls that fill the head of the valley at Blaen y Cwm.

This track goes westwards, and then turns to the north-west before heading south to cross a little stream. At this point you are about to leave the track altogether and make your way across the rough heathery moorland to the summit of **Cyrniau Nod**. Take a compass bearing for the summit which is 1½m away. ◄

At 666m Cyrniau Nod is the highest summit in the Hirnant range. Its name translates as 'mark cairns'.

A fence runs close by the summit and you should follow this north-west for 700m to a wide bull-dozed track. Turn right here and follow it to a big bend to the west. Just north of this a post marks the top of a little knoll. Walk over to this then on over very deep, pathless heather to the Bwlch y Dŵr, a broad, boggy col.

I passed this way during a two-month backpack in 1998 when I climbed all of the 2000 foot summits in Wales in one continuous expedition. It was a very wet and cold day and I traversed all of the Hirnants after a bad night camping wild in the Arans to the west. At one point on this crossing I sat down for a rest in the heather and awoke quite a while later freezing cold and close to hypothermia. These wild hills are not for the faint-hearted.

A vague ridge rises from here to the north-east, leading you eventually to the ling-covered summit dome of **Foel Cwm-Sian Llŵyd**. ▸

Walk from the summit north-westwards along a vague and very broad ridge leading over to a group of little knolls at Rhiwaedog-is-afon. You will see the dense forests of Cwm Hirnant to your left as you walk. Continuing over the tops of Rhiwaedog-is-afon the way leads down to Bwlch-y-fenni where a good track passes over the col. Turn right here and follow the track just east of north down to Tŷ Cerrig on the B4391. Turn right on the road, crossing a bridge on a sharp bend left and continuing to a sharp right after 500m. Here a public footpath leads downhill to join the B4402. Turn right along this road and you will find yourself coming to the bridge just outside **Llandderfel** where you will be spending the night.

Day Two: Post Gwyn and Glan-hafon

Start the day by turning back along the B4402 then immediately left up a steep little lane past Caecynddelw. Follow this up to a junction with the B4391 by a conifer plantation. Turn left again along the B road until the plantation on the left ends. Here a public bridleway heads

This, the 'bare hill of grey Jane's valley' is arguably the best summit in the Hirnant range. It gives fine views northwards over towards Foel Goch in the Arenigs. The summit is marked by an OS trig pillar and stands at 648m above sea level.

Pistyll Rhaeadr

east over the moor to a broad col between the small hills of Rhanneg and Carnedd Wen. Follow the path to the col, then straight over to the gurgling Afon Dinam. Cross this and make for the woods to the east, following the bridleway through around a long spur and down into Cwm Pennant. Turn right along the minor road that leads up the cwm and follow it to its end at Blaen-y-cwm. The route continues as a track leading up along the eastern side of the Nant Sgrin and out onto the open moorland below spot height 434m. Stay on the track until you get to the main road at the Milltir Gerrig.

The rough flanks of Post Gwyn lead away to the south-east from the road, but the way starts as a fairly good track making towards the distant ridge of the Berwyns. Follow the track for 2km, and then branch off to the right over open moorland to gain the ridge of **Post Gwyn**. Here the going is very difficult through thigh-deep heather, cotton grass bogs, and mossy mires. **Post Gwyn** has two summits and you should aim to the north side of the first one, and then make directly for the second which is the higher of the two. ▸

Continue along the ridge from the summit towards the distant hillside of Y Clogydd where the going gets a little easier underfoot, then down to a col where tracks pass over from Llangynog to the west into the Afon Rhaeadr to the east. Ignore these and keep to the heights to the summit of **Glan-hafon**, marked by a trig pillar at 607m.

The route continues eastwards towards a junction of tracks and from here you should take the one going eastwards down to Cefn-coch, turning right in the hamlet, passing the telephone box, the turning left at the T-junction. This lane will take you easily downhill back to **Llanrhaeadr-ym-Mochnant**.

Post Gwyn translates as 'white pillar', which is odd given the very brown, heathery nature of its slopes. The summit is marked by a small cairn atop a grassy mound at 665m.

13 – The Heights of the Berwyn Range

Total Distance:	55km
Daily Distances:	1) 32km 2) 23km
Maps:	OS Landranger, sheet 125 *Bala and Lake Vyrnwy, Berwyn*
Starting Point:	Start at the square in the charming little village of Llanrhaeadr-ym-Mochnant (grid ref. SJ 124 261)

Area Summary: The Berwyns have developed a reputation for being the roughest, toughest group of hills in Wales for the walker to attempt. This accolade belongs more fairly to the hills of the western Berwyns, or Hirnants, covered in the previous chapter. The main ridge of the Berwyns, although definitely heathery in places and boggy in others, is actually a delight to walk along, and the subsidiary ridges are no less enjoyable. The Berwyns themselves rise to the immediate south of the River Dee, (the Afon Dyfrdwy) and roll away into the heartlands of Mid Wales and the English border hills to the south.

Transport: There is no public transport to the start of this route

Accommodation and supplies: There are good B&Bs in Llanrhaeadr-ym-Mochnant. Try Rose Cottage (tel. 01691 780398) or Plas-y-Llan (tel. 01691 780236). There are shops here from which you can buy limited supplies, and also a couple of good pubs.

Overnight Options: Try the youth hostel in Cynwyd (tel. 01490 412814) or the farmhouse B&B at Fron Goch 1½miles south of the village (tel. 01490 440418).

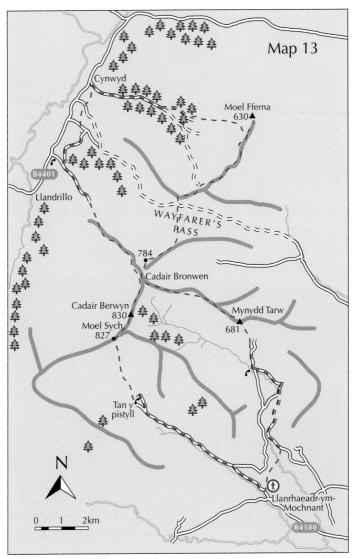

Map 13

Cynwyd

Moel Fferna
630▲

B4401

Llandrillo

WAYFARER'S
PASS

784●
Cadair Bronwen

Cadair Berwyn
830▲
Moel Sych
827●

Mynydd Tarw
681▲

Tan y
pistyll

N

0   1   2km

Llanrhaeadr-ym-
Mochnant

B4580

Walk Summary: A superb walk over little used tracks and paths along some of the best ridges in this part of Wales. The walking is occasionally off the beaten track however, and you really do need to have a feel for confident navigation to tackle these hills safely. The walk takes in all the main summits of the Berwyns range, bar Post Gwyn which lies out to the west and formed part of the previous walk in this book. The first day takes you over Mynydd Tarw to Cadair Bronwen, then north-eastwards to distant Moel Fferna where much heathery ground is encountered. Easy tracks take you down to the Dee at Cynwyd (grid ref. SJ 056 409) for the night. Day Two follows better tracks to the highest summits of the Berwyns before descending by the side of Pistyll Rhaeadr, a fantastic waterfall, back into the valleys. A great walk and one not to be missed.

Day One: Quiet Ways to Cadair Bronwen

By the little corner shop in **Llanrhaeadr-ym-Mochnant** take the lane that leads up the valley to Pistyll Rhaeadr.

Mynydd Tarw

Two hundred metres along this you should look for a public footpath on the right that climbs up through woods and heads just east of north to the farm at Henfache. Cross the minor road and make your way down to the Afon Twrch, crossing this via a footbridge and climbing up to the north-east to a track just west of the farm at Plas-yn-glyn. Turn left along this track and follow it for nearly 3km to a big bend in a minor lane at grid ref. SJ 128 302. Turn right along this lane and walk around the big bend and on to the farm at Tyn-y-ffridd. Here there is a junction on the left with a lane leading back to Llanrhaeadr-ym-Mochnant, and just beyond, by the farm buildings a lane on the right climbing up to Maes and Votty. Take this lane up through Maes, but look for a public byway on the left just before reaching Votty. Take this to gain the long south ridge of **Mynydd Tarw**. Climb up to the summit via the western side of a forestry plantation. ▸

Walk westwards from the summit along a heathery track, staying on the southern side of a fence at first. This leads down to a col, which is boggy at times, then up to the north-west to the double-topped hill of Foel Wen. Walk over the first top and on to the second, which is marked by a little rocky outcrop, thrusting out of a patch of grass among the heather.

The summit of Mynydd Tarw is a fine spot marked by a large cairn glowing with bright bilberry plants. The name means 'mountain of the bulls' and is at 681m.

The summit of Foel Wen is not easy to find, as there is no cairn marking the highest point. It lies at 691m. Look out for nesting wading birds here in the summer, as golden plover and dunlin can both often be seen with chicks in the vicinity, as can red grouse. I was walking over here once and disturbed a sleeping buzzard that was snoozing on a fence post.

Head north-west from Foel Wen down to another peaty col, then turn to the west and climb up alongside the fence to the summit of Tomle at 741m.

Tomle, not very encouragingly, translates as 'the mire'. This is fantastic viewpoint for the main ridge of the Berwyns which you will be traversing tomorrow. The view takes in the whole eastern face of the ridge from Moel Sych to Cadair Berwyn. Tomle's summit is also a great place to look out for the Berwyn berry, so called from its Welsh name 'mwyar Berwyn'. This is the only place in Wales where it can be found, although it is common in Scotland where it in called the cloudberry. It has white flowers with five petals and an orange edible fruit. The leaves look a little like those of a blackberry, although the plant grows very close to the ground.

Walk westward off Tomle down to a grassy col where the fence is crossed by an ancient track crossing the range. ◄

An ancient marker post can be found at the gate, although it is now recumbent.

Follow the public bridleway off the north side of the col, leading around on a contouring line to the Bwlch Maen Gwynedd, immediately south of the summit of

The Berwyns

Cadair Bronwen. Rough slopes of grass and heather lead easily up to the huge summit cairn at 784m.

A long ridge is thrown out to the north-east from the summit of Cadair Bronwen and this is the way that you should go. Start by following the compass in this direction, following a vague path at first. This soon brings you to a long heathery stretch with much peaty and boggy ground underfoot. A fence leads the way down to an inconspicuous minor summit on the ridge, where the vague path turns to the north and leads you onwards to the main track at a col 2km to the north.

The Wayfarers Pass is an old drovers route which actually got its name much more recently. There is a memorial on the top of the pass, just underneath a rock wall, marked as to 'A Wayfarer 1877–1956, Lover of Wales'. There is a visitor's book cached near to the memorial.

Climb up to the north from the memorial, crossing a fence and turning left alongside of it. This passes to the north of three small forestry plantations, then picks out a rough line through deep heather to a spot height at 592m. The fence leads the way throughout, making the going seem a little friendlier. Continue down from the spot height to a broad col, and then up via occasional rock steps to the nice little summit of Cerrig Coediog, also at 592m. Continue walking alongside the fence until you reach a good track which crosses the range. A short dash up the hillside to the north brings the nice little summit of **Moel Fferna** underfoot.

Return to the main track and turn right, westwards. This is a nice track that leads easily down to the valley of the River Dee at **Cynwyd**. The route takes you through delightful forestry and soon has you knocking at the door of the youth hostel where you will spend the night.

Day Two: The Main Ridge of the Berwyns

Start the day by taking the lane outside the hostel uphill towards the farm at Pen-y-felin. Turn right after 300m and follow it round to Colomendy then out to a junction. Straight ahead lies a narrow public footpath, which you should take through the fields to the farms at Cwm where a track cuts up the hill to the left. Take this steeply, then turn right at a junction and contour around to the house at Hendre. The track drops down to cross the beautiful waters of the Afon Llynor, and just beyond you should turn left along an old drover's track that leads you up towards the distant mountains. The way leads through fields at first, then by a couple of forestry plantations before taking to the broad pasturelands around Moel Pearce. Here the going becomes more rugged underfoot and as you climb around the north and western slopes of Cadair Bronwen, whose summit you scaled yesterday, the terrain turns to rough mountain grasses and hard rushes. The track soon leads to the Bwlch Maen Gwynedd, which you crossed yesterday. Turn right here and ignore the track on the left which leads over towards Tomle. Instead climb up the long northern ridge of Cadair Berwyn to gain the rim of the broken crags that fall away to the south-east. Handrail along these along a good path to the fine twin summits of **Cadair Berwyn**.

The summit of Cadair Berwyn, or the 'chair of Berwyn' is at 830m, although this is something that has only recently been realised. The old maps used to show that Moel Sych to the south was the highest summit of the range at 827m, while the second summit was marked as a point which still has an OS trig pillar. New surveys now show that the point with the trig pillar is much lower than Moel Sych, and that a point between the two is actually the highest summit of the range. Hence we now have a 'New Top of Cadair Berwyn', and 'Old Top' and Moel ▸

◂ Sych, all dotted along the ridge and each clamouring for the attention of the hillwalker. The first summit has an OS trig pillar marking its highest point, while just a little further south is the true summit at 830m.

The summit of Moel Sych lies just beyond a fence and is marked by a large cairn. The name translates as 'dry bare hill', though I can only assume that it was during a long spate of drought when the surveyors first named it.

Walk down to the south-west to a nice col where easy slopes lead you up to the summit of **Moel Sych** at 827m. Head south-east from the summit until you come to the top edge of a line of cliffs. Turn right along the rim and handrail down this fine ridge to a broad track that lies just above the superb waterfalls at Pistyll Rhaeadr. There is a viewing platform at the top of the falls, although the rock here can be slippery and there is thankfully no barrier to keep you back from the edge. Be very careful!

Turn right and follow the broad track down to the farm at little café at **Tan-y-pistyll**. ▸

Walk out along the lane from the café. This leads down the valley and will take you all the way to Llanrhaeadr-ym-Mochnant. It is an easy, pleasant walk along the tarmac, although it is 5km of road walking which can hard on the feet. Be careful at weekends if there is any traffic around – a visit to the falls is a popular excursion for many people staying in the area. Little more than an hour will see you back at **Llanrhaeadr-ym-Mochnant** and the end of a great wild walk.

The best views of the falls can be had from the small footbridge that crosses the river right underneath the main shoot. A path leads down to this from the gateway to the café.

14 – The Plynlimon Range
from Staylittle

Total Distance:	68km
Daily Distances:	1) 29km 2) 26km
	3) 13km
Maps:	OS Landranger, sheet 135 *Aberystwyth*
Starting Point:	Start in the tiny village of Staylittle, about midway between Llanidloes and Llanbrynmair on the B4518. Park sensibly in the village near the bridge (grid ref. SN 884 924)

Area Summary: A very wild and rugged mountain range, though Plynlimon, however, does come across as being a friendly sort of place for the walker and backpacker. The range is bounded to the south by the A44 from Rhayader to Aberystwyth, to the west by the Afon Rheidol and

Transport: There is not public transport into this wild corner of Wales

Accommodation and supplies: The only place to stay near the start of the walk is the fine Star Inn just along the road at Dylife (tel. 01650 521345). This is a popular place with walkers and real-ale drinkers. There is little else hereabouts, but the fleshpots of Llanidloes are not far to the south-east and Machynlleth lies not far away to the north. There are no shops here either, or on route, so bring supplies with you.

Overnight Options: On the first night you should make use of the fine forest bothy at Nantsyddion (grid ref. SN 773 791), while the small campsite at Rhiwgam, south of Machynlleth, provides somewhere to pitch a tent on the second night (grid ref. SN 797 948).

Nant-y-moch Reservoir, to the east by the dense forestry plantations of the Hafren Forest above Staylittle, and to the north by mile after mile of open moorland and yet more forestry, falling in deep cwms to the River Dovey at Machynlleth. Immediately north of the main summits of the range, the deep valley of the Afon Hengwm separates the high summit ridge from this wild landscape of heather and forest.

Walk Summary: This is a long walk through little-frequented country. Paths that exist are often very boggy, while much of the route crosses difficult deep heather and blanket bog. The going is tough, though not really rocky, and some of the views are among the best in the whole of Wales. This really is a route for the mountain connoisseur. Day One takes you along the stream of the Afon Clywedog before bashing across pathless heather to gain the main ridge of the Plynlimon range. The entire ridge is traversed before dropping down to the south and crossing the Afon Castell to find a bothy for the night. On day two you head north-west towards the Nant-y-moch Reservoir, climb three fine little summits clustered around it before heading north to the little camp site of Rhiwgam. On the final day you take a walk around the Glaslyn Nature Reserve before visiting a Roman Fort on your way back to Staylittle.

Plynlimon in winter

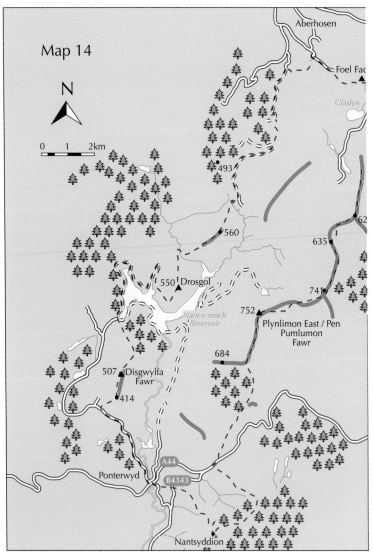

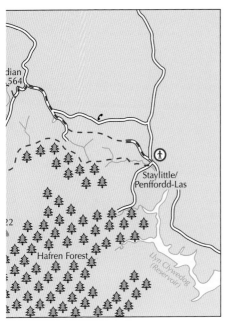

Day One: The Main Plynlimon Ridge Traverse

Start this walk by crossing the Afon Clywedog via the bridge on the minor road that leads towards the Hafren Forest via Llwynygog. Turn right along a track and follow it between two tumuli then down to the stream again where you re-cross to the northern side. ▶

Follow the track along the northern side of the valley, dropping down to the water level of the stream right at the head beyond some old mine workings. Cross over here and skirt around the western end of the forest to its south-western point. From here rough ground leads the way south-westwards up the long, easy-angled ridge of Carnfachbugeilyn. The summit is marked by an ancient cairn at 622m.

Follow the ridge to the south-west, taking a compass bearing in anything other than good visibility. Here you

Staylittle gets its name from the village blacksmith who was said to be able to shoe horses so quickly that his smithy became known as 'Stay-a-little'.

will pass close by the source of the River Severn. The source of the mighty river lies a little way over to the east, although it is not clear which of the many marshy pools and bogs is regarded as the true source.

Bear south for the top edge of a forestry plantation, and then continue onwards to the summit of Pen Pumlumon Arwystli at 741m. ◄

Pick up a line of boundary stones that head just south of west towards the summit of Plynlimon East Top, passing very close to the source of the River Wye.

> The source here is much more obvious than that of the River Severn, although to reach it you have to descend nearly 40m to the east. Note also that an alternative name for Plynlimon East Top is Pen Pumlumon Llygad-Bychan, which means 'five stacks top of the small stream source'.

Westwards again the fine, rocky top of **Pen Pumlumon Fawr**, the highest point of the range at 752m, rises above the bogs and pools. A large cairn adorns its top, along with an OS trig pillar.

Here you meet the main track up Plynlimon, which climbs out of the valleys to the south. Head along this for 2km to the top corner of a forest, then nip out to the west for the fine view across the Nant-y-moch Reservoir from Y Garn at 684m. Return the way you went along the forest boundary, then turn to the south-east along the main track, still skirting around the forests of Dyll Faen. A fantastic public footpath leads away to the south-west. Descend gradually to the old coaching inn at Dyffryn Castell. Turn right down the main road at the Dyffryn Castell for a short way, looking for a public footpath sign on the left after just 300m. This starts off somewhat incongruously, taking you through an old mine before finding a pleasant way up the west side of the Nant Meirch and over a fine ridge overlooking the

The Welsh spelling for Plynlimon is often given as Pumlumon, which means 'five summits', although it is not clear which of the many lumps and bumps along the ridge are the 'five'.

forests of the Afon Mynach. Drop over the other side of the ridge and enter the forest via the public footpath. This descends steeply to a stream above which you will come to a track junction. Turn right here and follow the main track along the north side of the Afon Melin for 2½km to a woodland clearing where the bothy of **Nantsyddion** lies. You should spend the night here.

Day Two: The Hills around the Nant-y-moch Reservoir

Start the day by heading back along the track you came in by the night before. After just 200m a junction is reached and you should turn left here, climbing uphill to yet another junction after a further 200m. Turn right and follow this track for 500m to where a public footpath leads westwards out of the forest and onto the open moor of Mynydd yr Ychen. Follow the public footpath to the north-west along a broad ridge, dropping down to the B4343 road just north of Parcgwyn. Cross straight over the road and pick up another public footpath dropping downhill beside a wood to the main road, the A4120, in **Ponterwyd**. Turn right here and walk out to the junction with the A44(T). Turn left, crossing the bridge, and then take the next lane on the right after the chapel. Follow this lane up into the forests of Banc Creignant Mawr, continuing along the lane as it emerges from the trees and dropping down to cross a little stream. Just beyond on the right there is an ancient standing stone 200m from the road, and you should make for this. Walk north-eastwards up the fine little hill of Disgwylfa Fach at 414m high, then turn to the north and drop down to a blanket bog col before tackling the steep southern ridge of **Disgwylfa Fawr**.

The summit here is marked by a large tumulus and stands at 507m above sea level. The origin of the name is not that easy to trace. It is thought that it ▸

‹ has a similar origin to the name Ddysgl, as in Crib y Ddysgl, that fine mountain of the Snowdon range. This is often given as meaning 'ridge of the dish', although W.P.Haskett Smith wrote in his book *Climbing in the British Isles* in 1895 that 'the common derivation of the name is from "destillare" – i.e. "dripping ridge"'. It is unlikely though that a wet ridge in Wales would be considered that unusual so as to give it its own name. Most ridges in Wales drip at some point or other most weeks! Haskett Smith goes on, 'Attempts to derive the name from "disgl" (dish) seem equally futile. Possibly the explanation may be found in the word "dysgwyl" (watch or expect) ... which would make it parallel to names like Lookingstead, etc.' So, we are left thinking that Disgwylfa Fawr probably means something along the lines of 'big look-out hill', but might derive from 'hill of the dish'. Certainly Crib y Ddysgl is more commonly called 'ridge of the dish today'.

Walk north from the summit of Disgwylfa Fawr to the corner of a forest on Bryn Gwyn. Turn to the north-west and follow the edge of the forest down to a little road on the banks of the Nant-y-moch Reservoir. Nant-y-moch means simply 'stream of the pigs'.

Turn left along the lane and follow it around to the north-westernmost point of the reservoir.

This is a great place to look for red-breasted merganser and goosander ducks, as well as oystercatchers, redshanks and common sandpipers in summer. Ospreys also stop off here on migration during the spring and autumn, and many local people feel sure that it is only a matter of time before they nest here. It would make a great spot for them!

Continue as the road enters the forest, the just before a cattle grid a track on the right leads off to the east and crosses the low southern ridge of Fainc Fawr. Continue along the track as it heads around the northern shore of the reservoir, until you reach the cackling stream of the Nant y Baracs. Cross here on a public bridleway which climbs around the southern flanks of the superb little hill of **Drosgol**. Follow the bridleway around to the southern ridge of the hill, then turn north and climb up to the summit at 550m. ▸

Turn north again and follow the rough slopes down to the banks of the Afon Llechwedd-mawr. You need to cross over this wide stream to gain the ridge of Banc Llechwedd-mawr to the north-east, but as it can be difficult to cross you may have to head quite a way upstream to find a safe crossing point. From the spot height 355m you should head east up the broad flank of Banc Llechwedd-mawr, gaining the ridge at point 543m and following it north-eastwards to the cairned summit at 560m. Drop off the summit to the north, making slightly to the east for the farmstead at Hyddgen where a bridge takes you over the stream to the track leading north into the dark forests of Mynydd Bychan. Walk north into the forest for just under one kilometre until you reach a stream. ▸

Cross the stream and head just north of east along a good track that stays close by the northern side of the stream, soon emerging from the forest and heading east over the ridge of Siambr Trawsfynyc. Here a not-so-obvious public footpath heads north over the range to come out at a good track just above Rhiwgam farm where you should camp for the night.

Day Three: Glaslyn Nature Reserve and Penycrocbren

Start this final day by heading off down the driveway to the farm, looking for a public bridleway on the right just as you enter some small woods after 600m. Turn right along this and cross the stream just 300m down to pick

The name Drosgol translates simply as 'rough ground'. No understatement here! A couple of fine cairns mark the top.

These forests are one of the best places in Wales to see those great little birds the siskins, redpolls and crossbills. These are all types of finches, each brightly coloured, and each fills its own niche in the forest.

up a public footpath that leads back up the hill on the other side to Rhosygarreg. Another public footpath heads off downhill to the north-east of the farm here, crossing another stream known as the Afon Dulas, before climbing up to the public road at Nantyfyda. Just before reaching the public road a track leads off up the hill to the right. This is the route taken by the long-distance footpath Glyndŵr's Way. Turn right along this and follow it up above a fine gorge below Foel Fadian. Just beyond the gorge you reach a good track where you should turn left and take the track that leads to and circles the **Glaslyn** Nature Reserve.

> The gorge is a good place in which to see peregrine falcons, as they often nest hereabouts, while the waters of Glaslyn hold some breeding ducks and waders. The moors here may be a good place to look for short-eared owls and hen harrier, while the smaller birds of the moor, meadow pipits, stonechats and wheatears are very common.

Return along the track to regain Glyndŵr's Way and follow it out to a minor road. Turn right along this and continue until a footpath on the right leads down a track, also taken by Glyndŵr's Way, to cross a tiny stream below a little tarn. Climb up the other side to gain the hill of Penycrocbren with its Roman Fortlet, and continue back to **Staylittle** by heading east all the way on Glyndŵr's Way.

15 – Pen y Garn and Cwmystwyth

Total Distance:	48km
Daily Distances:	1) 24km 2) 24km
Maps:	OS Landranger, sheet 135 *Aberystwyth*
Starting Point:	The picnic site car park in the tiny hamlet of Crosswood, on the B4340 north-west of Pontrhydfendigaid (grid ref. SN 667 728).

Area Summary: A lovely area of mid-Wales, the region around Cwmystwyth is a green and pleasant land. Deep wooded valleys rise to low, forested hills, and the area is well-served by dozens of minor roads linking small villages and hamlets. This is the area around Devil's Bridge, east of Aberystwyth.

Walk Summary: A truly great walk of varied scenery, lots of wildlife, and good paths. This route is suitable for

Transport: There is no public transport to the start of this route

Accommodation and supplies: Although there is nowhere to stay in Crosswood, there is certainly no shortage of guesthouses, B&Bs and the like in Aberystwyth just to the west. This is also the place to stock up on food for your trip. There are a few shops and cafes in Devil's Bridge on day one, and an inn at Pont-rhyd-y-groes on Day Two.

Overnight Options: Use the bothy at Nant Rhys, deep in the forests north of Cwmystwyth (grid ref. SN 837 793). There are also campsites in Cwmystwyth itself, although you would have to make Day One's walk much longer in order to get there, and so the walk on Day Two would be much shorter.

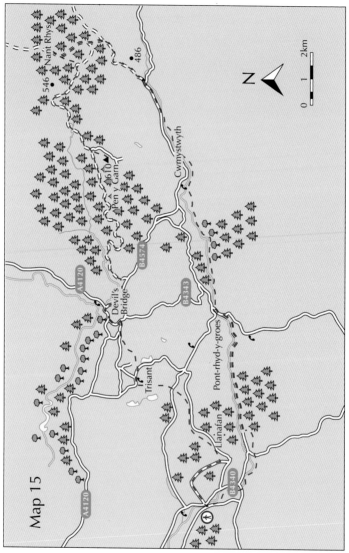

Map 15

546 Nant Rhys

486

Cwmystwyth

610 Pen y Garn

B4574

A4120

B4343

Devil's Bridge

Trisant

Pont-rhyd-y-groes

Llanafan

A4120

B4340

N

0 1 2km

those with little backpacking experience, as the distances covered each day are not too great, there is not too much height gain during each day's walk, and the overnight stop-over is at a bothy, so there's no need to carry a tent. The walk starts by making for Devil's Bridge over the low hills between the rivers Rheidol and Ystwyth, then heads east for the summit of Pen y Garn. The bothy at Nant Rhys, just east of Pen y Garn is used overnight. On Day Two you will head south into the deep trench of Cwmystwyth, then turn westwards and follow the valley down stream back to Crosswood.

Day One: Devil's Bridge and Pen y Garn

Start the day by walking out of the car park onto the main road and turning right over the bridge. Turn left immediately and then right at the next turning. This is a good track leading up and around the back of Trawsgoed, and then curving to the south-east to Talgarth. Just beyond Talgarth a public footpath on the left takes you uphill towards a nice woodland above the village of Llanafan and you should follow this path to the north-east keeping above but parallel to the minor road. Eventually you turn to the east below the spot height 295m and, staying parallel to the road pass beneath a little knoll before dropping down off the hill to the north-east to cross the cheerful stream of Nant Cwmnewydion. ▸

Cross the stream and follow the path northwards to come out at a minor road at Cwmnewydion Uchaf farm. Dead ahead a public footpath leads into a wood and you should follow this along the west bank of a little stream up to Nantgwyn Farm, continuing onwards to Rhosrhydd at another minor road. Turn right here, and then take the next on the left on the lane down to Mynydd Bach where you come to a T-junction. Take the lane to the right and continue eastwards out to the B4343 road where you should turn left and walk down the hill into the village of **Devil's Bridge**. Turn right on the A4120 to get to the bridges.

This is a great place to see beautiful and banded demoiselles during the summer months. These are dark blue and bottle green damselflies, and can be seen through much of mid-Wales around shady streams and ponds.

There are three bridges at Devil's Bridge, all built pretty much one on top of the other. The lower bridge has actually been dated as being medieval, the middle one being from the 18th century and the one we now use when we drive along the A4120 was built during the 19th century. There is a small charge for viewing the bridges from either side of the road.

The story goes that a lonely old lady called Marged once lived by the Afon Mynach with her dog Smala, and her cow Malen. One day Malen somehow strayed across the river. Because of the steep-sided gorge here, Marged couldn't get across to bring her back. The Devil appeared, disguised as a monk and by way of a deal, said that in return building a bride over the river, he would have the first living thing to cross it as his own. He obviously had designs on Marged herself, hoping she would cross to fetch the cow. She agreed, and threw a crust of bread over the new bridge that the Devil had built. Smala scampered over after the crust, and the Devil became the proud owner of a flee-bitten mutt while Marged got her cow back.

By the hotel overlooking the bridges there is a road junction, the B4574. Leave Devil's Bridge by walking along this, climbing uphill for nearly 1km until you come to a track on the left taken by a public footpath. Take this path along the south side of the beautiful Afon Mynach, entering the forests after 1½km. Climbing up-hill through the forest you will come to a junction, turn right here and follow the good track as it winds its way around the northern slopes of the little hill called Truman. You should gain the main track through the forest just to the east of the little knoll shown as being 480m high. Turn left along the main track, gaining fine views across the valley to the north as you get to the small clearing at Banc yr Adarn. ◄

The view from Banc yr Adarn takes in the whole of the Plynlimon range to the north, while nearer at hand common buzzards can be seen soaring above the wooded valley of the upper Afon Mynach.

Soon the track emerges from the trees as you continue eastwards. Up on the right is the little summit of **Pen y Garn**, and you will come to a track on the right heading gently uphill to its top after 500m. Take this track directly to the summit at 610m above sea level. The top of **Pen y Garn** is adorned with solar panels and botany monitoring equipment, as well as a large cairn and an OS trig pillar.

Return northwards along the path to the main track and turn right towards the lonely farmstead of Cripiau Nantmelyn. Just before reaching the farm itself a junction takes you off to the right, eastwards again and back into the forests. ▸

The track takes you north towards the western slopes of Banc Nant-rhys, then skirts this little ridge to its south side and plunges deep into the forest around the slopes of Bryn Rhudd. Here you will come to a not-very-obvious public footpath leading just east of north towards the little bothy of **Nant Rhys**. If you should miss this footpath continue onwards along the main track down to the river and just turn left following it upstream to the bothy after 2km. Spend the night here in the bothy, taking your water from the nearby Afon Diliw.

Look out for siskins, redpoll, crossbills and warblers here in the forests.

Day Two: Cwmystwyth

Leave the bothy by making for the Afon Diliw and following its peat-stained waters downstream, passing the end of the track that you came in by last night and onwards to a lane that cuts across the range from north-east to

Banded Demoiselle in Cwmystwyth

south-west. The best track down to this point is on the western side of the river. Turn right and follow the lane south-westwards, across rough moorland at first then into a steep-sided valley between the hills of Lan Fawr and Yr Allt. The track then takes you down to Blaenycwm in the beautiful valley of **Cwmystwyth**.

For nature lovers this is one of the best places in mid-Wales to see the red kite, that fantastic bird of prey that was on the very of extinction in Britain at the turn of the 20th century. Just a couple of pairs survived in mid-Wales, and a concerted effort by a handful of dedicated ornithologists saw it come back from the brink and re-colonise vast parts of the country. More recent introductions in England and Scotland have helped this magnificent raptor to spread throughout the whole of Britain.

Turn right down the valley for just over a kilometre, walking along the quiet lane past Tyllwyd to Tŷ-Mawr. ◄

At Tŷ-Mawr you should cross over the river via the bridge and pick up the path that leads downstream on the south side of the river. This is a beautiful part of the walk and is not to be rushed. The path leads on to Tynewydd where you should turn right on the lane and make for the bridge over the river. Just before crossing the bridge, a track on the left continues downstream and you should follow this through the farm at Dol-chenog and on into woods at Dologau where another bridge offers to take you over to the north bank.

Look for dippers, yellow wagtails and common sandpipers on the rocks in the riverbed, as well as peregrine falcons and buzzards in the skies overhead.

There are otters on the river in Cwmystwyth, although you would be very lucky to catch sight of any. The Eurasian otter, lutra lutra has evolved to live different lives according to its habitat. Those by the sea in Scotland are ruled by the tides, coming out ►

on a rising tide, whereas those inland through-out Britain are largely nocturnal, being ruled by the night. Many people erroneously believe that we have 'sea otters' and 'river otters' in Britain, but they are in fact the same species.

From Dologau ignore the bridge and stay on the path along the south bank of the river. This starts by crossing a meadow, and then plunges into a forest below Bryn Mawr. Keep to the path nearest to the river and follow it for 3km into the village of **Pont-rhyd-y-groes**. There are a few shops and an inn here for the weary.

Turn left along the road into the village, then right along the lane just beyond the chapel. This lane stays close by the river throughout, and you can either follow this or take to the forest walks up on the bank to the left. These run parallel to the road, so there is not much difference, other than your own preference for woodland walking or riverside walking.

After nearly 6km you will come to a junction with the B4340. Turn left along this for 300m, and then turn right down the track for Pen-y-bont. Walk over the little stream, and then bear right onto the public footpath that leads down to the southern bank of the Afon Ystwyth. This track leads around a couple of long bends all the way back to the car park in Crosswood where you started this walk.

16 – The Elan Valley Reservoirs

Total Distance:	43km
Daily Distances:	1) 21km 2) 22km
Maps:	OS Explorer, sheet 200 *Llandrindod Wells and the Elan Valley*
Starting Point:	The visitor centre car park at the eastern end of Caban-coch Reservoir. This is reached from Rhayader town centre by taking the road westwards into the Elan Valley (grid ref. SN 927 646).

Area Summary: A wild and remote-feeling area of low hills and moorland, stretching for mile after mile as a series of blanket bogs, rough grasses and deep gullies. The Elan Valleys lie to the immediate west of the town of Rhayader in mid-Wales, and are bounded to the north by Cwmystwyth and to the south by the main Builth Wells

Transport: It is possible to get to Rhayader by bus from most of the towns and villages in this area, although there is no service up the Elan Valley itself. The starting point for this walk lies 5km away from the centre of Rhayader.

Accommodation and supplies: There are lots of places to stay in Rhayader, as well as plenty of shops to buy supplies for this walk. Try the B&B at Brynteg on East Street (tel. 01597 810052), or there is a B&B, campsite and official red kite watching spot at Gigrin Farm (tel. 01597 810243). The tourist office can advise otherwise (tel. 01597 810591).

Overnight Options: Camp wild at Llyn Cerigllwydion Uchaf, north of the Claerwen Reservoir (grid ref. SN 840 692).

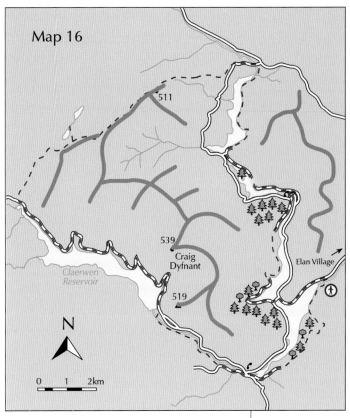

to Llandovery road, the A483. South again lies the out-of-bounds MOD property of the Mynydd Epynt.

Walk Summary: This is one of my own favourite areas for hillwalking, and backpacking in particular. The going is often tough, and you can feel a long way from anywhere and anybody on these wild moors, but this walk is an easy introduction to the area, and to backpacking with a tent. There are paths throughout much of the walk, all of which are straightforward to follow, and the views and wildlife are superb. On Day One you will skirt around the large Caban-coch and Claerwen Reservoirs, using the fantastic river of the Afon Claerwen as a means of linking the two. While on Day Two you head north across open moorland for Craig Goch Reservoir and then head south for Penygarreg and Garreg-ddu Reservoirs before heading back to the car. This is mainly a low to mid-level walk.

Day One: Around the Caban-Coch and Claerwen Reservoirs

Before starting this walk have a look in the Elan Valley Visitor Centre at the car park. It is mainly a permanent exhibition on the influence of the Victorian English on the flooding of the Elan Valley to give us the reservoirs that this walk takes you around. The emphasis is on how important the reservoir water was to the city of Birmingham in the 19th century. It goes on to say how wonderful the reservoirs are now to wildlife and the environment, and even states that some of the water is now drunk in Wales. It is true, the reservoirs are lovely, and the wildlife here is fantastic, but I feel that the valleys that were here before were probably much nicer, and that the wildlife would have been all the better for it. W.P.Haskett Smith wrote in his *Climbing in the British Isles* that Cwm Elan 'is a very pretty spot, and the gorge of Cefn Coch is exceedingly striking. Mackintosh says that the height is not less than 800 feet, and the cliffs are in many parts mural and quite perpendicular. He declared that, while the cliffs on the left-hand side of the river are very fine, he had seen nothing to surpass those on the right. This from a hill traveller of his experience is remarkably high praise ... The Birmingham reservoir is to submerge several miles of this cwm.'

Start the walk by heading west along the river from the car park, crossing over to the south bank at a footbridge underneath the dam of the reservoir. A public footpath leads up the hill, and then you should turn back to the west and walk to the dam itself. From here a footpath takes you around the southern shore of Caban-coch Reservoir for 1km until you reach a wood by a waterfall.

In 1892 the local people fought for the right of unrestricted access to these hills upon the building of the first reservoir in the Elan Valley, and an act was passed in parliament giving the freedom of these lovely hills to anyone who wanted to enjoy 'air, exercise and recreation'. This applies to any unenclosed land, of which there is no shortage in these hills.

Follow the path as it turns sharply uphill alongside the wood, continuing to Ty'n-y-pant where you should walk around the back of a little conifer plantation and head west towards a stream. Cross this via a ford, and continue westwards, along a public bridleway now to the top edge of the wood. Follow this track across two more streams, then downhill to the banks of the small Dolymynach Reservoir.

This is a great place to look out for common sandpipers in summer. These little wading birds nest by the banks of lakes and streams in upland areas. They are basically brown above and white underneath, and have an obvious white bar running in front of each wing. They can often be heard piping in high-pitched tones as they fly away upon your approach.

Continue along the bridleway and out to a tarmac lane by a bridge. Do not cross the bridge however, but stay on the south bank of the river. Walk along the road

147

to Rhiwnant where the tarmac ends. Turn right by the farm buildings, picking up a public byway that crosses fields by the Afon Claerwen.

> Look out for dippers here on the river. They are like little blackbirds with a white breast, and can dive underwater for food. They have specially adapted toes to help them cling to the riverbed, aiding them as they walk along the bottom in search of food.

The byway continues along the south side of the river to a side stream, the Afon Arban. Ford this and walk out to another little road. Cross the bridge via this road, then turn off to the left and climb the bank beside the dam to the eastern tip of the **Claerwen Reservoir**. Follow this byway all the way around the northern shore of the reservoir, until you reach the western end after nearly nine kilometres.

> The hills around the reservoirs here are some of the Welsh strongholds of the red kite. This large bird of prey used to be a common site throughout Britain, especially in our towns and cities where it would scavenge around rubbish dumps and tips. It was driven to the verge of extinction by man until, by the turn of the 20th century, only a pair remained. These were nesting in the Tywi Valley, over to the south-west of Claerwen. The birds were protected from poisoning and egg thieves by the bird watchers of the day, and now they have succeeded in bringing themselves back from the brink of extinction to become one of the most common birds of prey in mid-Wales. The RSPB have reintroduced them elsewhere in Britain, and they can now be seen in large numbers in the Chilterns, Yorkshire, and Northumberland and in Dumfries and Galloway, Stirlingshire and on the Black Isle in Scotland.

Just before reaching Claerwen farm a track climbs up the hillside on the right. This is an old route known as Esgair Gwar-y-tŷ. Follow this over rough moorland to the north-east, continuing as you gain a rough ridge where another byway comes in from the left. Turn right at this junction and follow the byway around the head of the little cwm holding the stream of Ddwynant. The route climbs again to a spot height at 542m, and just north of this point a rocky area has the lonely moorland tarn of Llyn Cerrigllwydion Uchaf just beyond. Walk over the rocky ground to the edge of the tarn and camp here for the night.

Day Two: Over Carn Ricet to the Craig Goch Reservoir

Start the day by heading back to the track and turn eastwards along this. The route continues along this track over many rough kilometres of moorland. First it swings around the vague ridge of Waun Bryn-hir before heading towards the north-east alongside an old water course. The ridge then becomes more defined as you

Winter in the Elan Valley

near Clawdd-du-bach and you should continue to the little hill of Carn Ricet at 511m. The cairn that gives this hill its name lies a little further on along the track.

Continue walking along the track and as you start to descend off Carn Ricet, keep with it as it turns more eastwards and dips along the head of the cwm holding Nant Torclawdd. Below is a road, running along the western side of Craig Goch Reservoir, and your track continues north-eastwards until you reach it at 348m. Turn left along this road and cross the Afon Elan at the Pont yr Elan. Leave the road here and walk south along the river as it flows into the Craig Goch Reservoir. There is a bit of a path underfoot as you skirt around its eastern shore, but it's not until you reach the car park and road at the dam of the reservoir that things underfoot improve drastically. At the dam a public bridleway takes you southeast through fine deciduous woodlands of oak and birch. Below on your right is the Penygarreg Reservoir, and you soon drop down to its shores. Within a short time you will reach the dam for this reservoir and you should continue out to another tarmac lane. Cross the bridge via the road leading towards a car park and follow it to a sharp bend right. At the bend a public footpath leaves the road and takes you south along the western side of yet another reservoir, the Garreg-ddu. This footpath stays a good way above the reservoir as it makes its way to Tynllidiart where you cross fields and a stream before continuing south and around the lower slopes of the tree-covered ridge of Glannau. Follow the public footpath around to cross the gushing waters of the Nant Methan, then on and around into a large bay of the reservoir to cross another stream. From here the path takes you eastwards to a public road. Turn left along this, walking across the bridge that separates the Garreg-ddu Reservoir from the Caban-coch Reservoir. ◄

At the far side there is a junction where you should turn right and follow the road around the northern side of the Caban-coch back to your car.

This bridge sits atop a submerged dam. Water is extracted from the reservoirs via the Foel Tower just north of the bridge, from where it feeds Birmingham with water. The city is 118km away and the water is gravity fed along the pipes. A fall of 51m is required.

17 – The Cwmdeuddwr Hills

Total Distance:	38km
Daily Distances:	1) 23km 2) 15km
Maps:	OS Explorer, sheet 200 *Llandrindod Wells and the Elan Valley*
Starting Point:	The centre of Rhayader town (grid ref. SN 972 680)

Area Summary: A wild and remote-feeling area of low hills and moorland, stretching for mile after mile as a series of blanket bogs, rough grasses and deep gullies. The Elan Valley lie to the immediate west of the town of Rhayader in mid-Wales, and are bounded to the north by Cwmystwyth and to the south by the main Builth Wells to Llandovery road, the A483. South again lies the out-of-bounds MOD property of the Mynydd Epynt.

Walk Summary: This is one of the very best backpacking areas in Wales because, although the going is often

Transport:	It is possible to get to Rhayader by bus from most of the towns and villages in this area. Telephone the tourist office for details on 01597 810591.
Accommodation and supplies:	There are lots of places to stay in Rhayader, as well as plenty of shops to buy supplies for this walk. Try the B&B at Brynteg on East Street (tel. 01597 810052), or there is a B&B, campsite and official red kite watching spot at Gigrin Farm (tel. 01597 810243). The tourist office can advise otherwise (tel. 01597 810591).
Overnight Options:	Camp wild in the quiet valley of the Nant y Gadair, beside the stream that flows south into the Claerwen Reservoir (grid ref. SN 868 663).

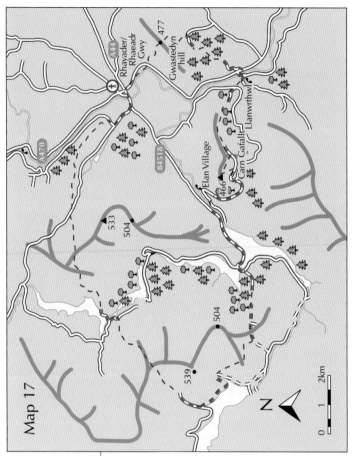

Map 17

477
Rhayader/
Rhaeadr
Gwy
Gwastedyn
hill
A44
A470
B4518
Elan Village
Carn Gafallt
Llanwrthwl
466
533
504
504
539
N
0   1   2km

tough, and you can feel a long way from anywhere and anybody on these wild moors, the views and wildlife are magnificent throughout. On Day One you will head south from Rhayader for the little bump of Gwastedyn Hill where hundreds of red kites can be seen circling overhead, waiting for feeding time at Gigrin Farm below, the onwards to cross the River Wye before making for the Caban-coch Reservoir. From here you'll head west for the high moors of Craig Fawr, finding a wild-camping spot in one of the many steep-sided valleys of this range. On day two you'll cross the moors to the north, before picking up a public bridleway that leads back towards Rhayader. This is a very tough walk, although quite short, and you will need to be well practised at map and compass work before setting off over these bare hills.

Day One: Gwastedyn Hill, Carn Gafallt and Craig Fawr

Leave **Rhayader** along the main road (A470(T)) running southwards from the centre of town towards Builth Wells. Where a big bend in the River Wye after 400m brings the river close by the road, take a public footpath that leads down to its eastern bank and follow it for a short way back out onto the road again.

The river here is a great place to watch for otters. In fact they are occasionally seen from the bridge right in the middle of Rhayader town itself. However, they are pretty much nocturnal only, so you would be very lucky to see one during daylight hours.

Cross the main road and look for a public bridleway on the right. This leads uphill alongside the RSPB's Dyffryn Wood Nature Reserve. Wood warblers, redstarts and pied flycatchers are among the birds that are widely regarded as being specialities of mid-Wales. They arrive during the early summer to breed in ancient oak woodlands such as those here at Dyffryn.

The public bridleway climbs up to the east of the fine little hill of **Gwastedyn**. You can detour off to the right to climb to its summit.

From the summit of Gwastedyn Hill you look down upon Gigrin Farm where there is an official red kite feeding station. This large bird of prey used to be a common site throughout Britain, especially in our towns and cities where it would scavenge around rubbish dumps and tips. It was driven to the verge of extinction by man, until by the turn of the 20th century only a pair remained. These were in the Tywi Valley, over of the moors to the west of Rhayader. The birds were protected from poisoning and egg thieves by the bird watchers of the day, and now they have succeeded in bringing themselves back from the brink of extinction to become one of the most common birds of prey in mid-Wales. Certainly standing on Gwastedyn Hill you should see them circling over Gigrin, waiting for feeding time. Around noon each day it is not unusual to see well over 100 kites in the air above the farm here. You can pay a small fee to go into one of the hides at Gigrin and watch the kites scavenging on the meat that the owner throws out for them. This is also a good place to watch buzzards and members of the crow family, while the farm also has woodland birds and badgers.

Follow the public bridleway over the hill to Pen-y-ffynnon, the west into the woods of Caerhyddwen. You come out into a clearing at a junction of tracks, and should be careful to take the right-hand one, heading just south of west over a little stream as it re-enters the wood. It emerges from the trees after a short way, about 600m, and then curves around to the farm at Ashfield. Walk south along the track from the farm into Ashfield Wood, and look out for a public footpath leaving the bridleway on the right. This leads down to the A470. Bear right to a road junction and turn off the main road over a bridge to **Llanwrthwl**. Follow the road to the right through the village, ignore the lane on the left then just 50m further on a track branches off the lane to the right. This is taken by the Wye Valley Walk long-distance trail and you should follow it north-westwards towards Dolgai. The route crosses a minor road here, then you continue uphill along the track through woods to Cefn, above which you emerge onto the eastern end of the little hill known as **Carn Gafallt**. The bridleway bears left, just south of west around the northern slopes of a little un-named hill at 419m, then continues to a junction of bridleways. From here you should leave the track altogether and aim for the summit of Carn Gafallt at 455m. ▸

Turn to the south-east and take a bearing for the cairns marked on the map above Coed Bwlch-glas. Here you come to a boundary running outside a little wood above the farm. Turn downhill alongside this, heading through the trees to pick up the bridleway at Coed Bwlch-glas. Turn right along this and walk out to the little lane at Pen y Castell. Turn right along the lane and follow it for 1km in a curve until you're beneath Allt Ddu woods. Here a public footpath leads downhill on the left through Cnwch Woods to a bridge leading over the Afon Elan to the Elan Valley Visitor Centre.

The views from the summit of Carn Gafallt are superb, taking in the trench of the Elan Valley with its reservoirs.

Walking above Rhayader

As well as a tourist information centre this is mainly a permanent exhibition on the influence of the Victorian English on the flooding of the Elan Valley to give us the reservoirs that this walk takes you around. The emphasis is on how important the reservoir water was to the city of Birmingham in the 19th century.

Gain the road above the visitor centre and turn west along this, walking along the northern side of the Caban-coch Reservoir to a junction where a road on the right crosses a bridge. ◄

This bridge sits atop a submerged dam. Water is extracted from the reservoirs via the Foel Tower just north of the bridge, from where it feeds water to Birmingham, 118km away. The water is gravity fed along the pipes, and a fall of 51m is required.

Cross the bridge and turn left for a 100m. On the right a public bridleway will take you straight up the hill through Llanerchi Wood and out to the radio masts on the little hill of Cefn Llanerchi at 440m above sea level. Drop down along the track to the west, crossing the little stream of the Llwydnant before continuing for 700m to a broad col at spot height 416m. Here you should leave the track altogether and make for the rocks above and to the right beneath the little hill at 504m (un-named). Climb easily around the right-hand side of the rocks to gain this boggy top, then skirt along the small escarpment on the left to the head of a stream from where you should take a bearing across the rough moorland to the summit of Craig Fawr at 519m. There is no path to the top, but there is a small cairn there. ◄

In 1892 the local people fought for the right of unrestricted access to these hills upon the building of the first reservoir in the Elan Valley, and an act was passed in parliament giving the freedom of these lovely hills to all. This applies to any unenclosed land.

From the summit of Craig Fawr take a bearing to the north-west to bring you out at the point where the tiny stream of Dyfnant flows into the huge Claerwen Reservoir. Here you'll come across a good public byway and should turn right along it around a little peninsular jutting into the reservoir and on to the next inlet at Nant y Gadair. A track leaves the byway here and makes its way up the east side of the stream, and you should follow this up to a confluence of stream where you should camp for the night.

Day Two: Esgair Perfedd and Maen-Serth

Start the day by following the main stream uphill to a very broad and boggy col between the rough moors of Craig Dyfnant to the south and Trumau to the north-west. The col is marked on the OS map at Y Groes at 496m (grid ref. SN 877 670). Walk north-east from the col along the broad, pathless ridge of Esgair Brithgwm and downhill to the north to the gurgling brook of Nant Gris. There are a few nice little waterfalls in Nant Gris.

Turn downhill and follow the stream down to the road above Penygarreg Reservoir. Turn left along the road to the dam, and walk along this to a car park and picnic site. A public bridleway leaves the road on the left just beyond the dam and climbs steadily uphill to the moorland heights of Esgair Perfedd. Cross this on the bridleway heading east towards the Roman Camp at the headwaters of the Nant Gwynllyn. Continue out to the road. ▸

Turn right along the road for 150m, then left off it along the continuation of the public bridleway. This leads eastwards along a fine ridge, marked by cairns to the standing stone of Maen-serth. You join a public byway just before reaching the stone, turning right along this. Follow the byway south-eastwards off the ridge, gaining fantastic views of Rhayader as you descend. The byway soon brings you out at a narrow lane, and you should turn right here down to a junction. Turn left and follow the road down to the main road leading from Rhayader into the Elan Valley. Turn left and follow it into town.

There is little see of the Roman Camp today, although you can pick out a few earthworks here and there.

The name Rhayader comes from Rhaeder Gwy, which means the 'waterfall on the Wye'. The town itself was the centre of the 'Rebecca Riots' in the mid-19th century when local farmers dressed themselves up as women in order to demolish the local tollgates which were prohibitively expensive for them and other local workers. It is a fine little town, and is the main centre for exploring the hills in this area and the Elan Valley itself.

18 – To the Source of the Afon Tywi

Total Distance:	44km
Daily Distances:	1) 27km 2) 17km
Maps:	OS Explorer, sheet 200 *Llandrindod Wells and the Elan Valley*
Starting Point:	The little car park near Tŷ-mawr, reached on the minor road from Beulah, west of Builth Wells, to Abergwesyn (grid ref. SN 859 531)

Area Summary: A very wild and rough area of low hills and moorland, stretching for mile after mile as a series of blanket bogs, rough grasses and deep gullies. The two high hills of the area, Drygarn Fawr and Gorllwyn, lie to the immediate south-west of the town of Rhayader in mid-Wales, and are bounded to the north by Cwmystwyth and to the south by the main Builth Wells to Llandovery road, the A483. South again lies the out-of-bounds MOD property of the Mynydd Epynt.

Transport: There is no public transport to the start of this walk

Accommodation and supplies: There are lots of places to stay in Rhayader, as well as plenty of shops to buy supplies for this walk. Try the B&B at Brynteg on East Street (tel. 01597 810052), or there is a B&B, campsite and official red kite watching spot at Gigrin Farm (tel. 01597 810243). The tourist office can advise otherwise (tel. 01597 810591). For great food try the Red Lion Inn in Llanafan-fawr, east of Beulah on the main road.

Overnight Options: Spend the night at the little bothy of Moel-prysgau, by the River Towy (Afon Tywi) (grid ref. SN 806 611).

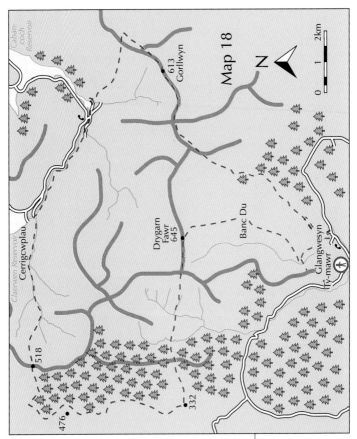

Walk Summary: This is one of the hardest walks in this book. The Abergwesyn hills are among the very best back-packing areas in Wales. Although the going is often tough, and you can feel a long way from anywhere and anybody on these wild moors, the views and wildlife are magnificent throughout. On Day One you will head north-east for the summit of Gorllwyn, then down into the Elan Valley to the north. From there public bridleways lead westwards over the hills to the source of the Afon Tywi via very wet ground. You will stay the night in a bothy deep in the forest by the river itself. On Day Two you take to the high ground again, making eastwards to Drygarn Fawr, then follow a broad ridge south back to your car. You will need to be well practised at map and compass work before setting off over these featureless hills.

Day One: The Abergwesyn Common and Gorllwyn

Start the day by walking along the narrow lane eastwards towards **Tŷ -mawr**. Pass the entrance to their driveway and cross a stream. Just beyond the stream you will come to a public footpath on the left which leads across a field to a bridleway. This will take you to **Glangwesyn** and up the eastern side of the little valley holding Nant Henfron through a great little woodland. ◄

Continue along the track, which is still a public bridleway, up to Carreg Lŵyd, then across to the northeast alongside a fence to a ford over a stream. Continue around the bottom edge of two field boundaries, then on to a crossing of the Nant Tŷ-coch. The bridleway takes you around the lower slopes of **Banc Du** as it makes its way north-eastwards to the forests of Cefn Garw. Head into the forest, taking the left-hand turning at the two junctions you come across, finally emerging onto the Abergwesyn Common below the little hill of Carnau, above the fine rocky gorge of the Nant Gewyn.

These woods are a good place for the nature lover to see redstarts, pied flycatchers and wood warblers in summer, while the stream's sides are good for grey wagtail.

> In 1984 the National Trust made the announcement that they had bought the 16,500 acres of land that make up the Abergwesyn Common, the area to the south of the Elan Valley Estates. The purchase was made with grants from the then Countryside Commission and the National Heritage Memorial Fund. This means you can wander anywhere you like around these fantastic moorlands and hills.

Continue along the bridleway to the rocky little area known as Carnau. The name literally means 'cairns' or 'stones'.

Walk on to the north-east along the track for a short way to the very boggy and broad col of Bwlch y Ddau Faen. From here you should follow a bearing eastwards along a broad ridge, marked occasionally by old boundary stones, to the summit of **Gorllwyn**. ▸

Continue along the ridge to the north-east, still vaguely following the line of boundary stones, to the moorland tarn of Llyn y Ferlen.

Gorllwyn is one of the main hills in this range, rising to 613m. The name means 'above the grove'. Its top is marked by a cairn and OS trig pillar.

These moors are a great place for nesting waders. I have seen golden plover and dunlin here in the summer, and occasionally see red kites flying over the area looking for carrion. On one occasion I was crossing these hills with a group when we found the prints of what could only be a badger. He must have been a long way from his sett.

Just beyond Llyn y Ferlen you come to a public bridleway, not terribly obvious on the ground, which leads down to the north-west to the western end of the **Caban-coch Reservoir**. The route is not obvious, but you should follow the broad ridge of Waun Lwyd, then down through fields to a farm near the stream of Nant Ddu. A public bridleway runs along the south side of the reservoir, so you'll hit that eventually. Turn left along the bridleway and follow it westwards out to a little minor road by a bridge. Do not cross the bridge, but walk westwards along the road to its end at Rhiwnant. At Rhiwnant you come across a public byway that leads down to the fantastic river of the Afon Claerwen. ▸

Walk along the southern bank of the Afon Claerwen for 3km to another road at Cerrigcwplau. Here you cross the Afon Arban at a ford. Turn left along a public bridleway which runs along the north side of the Afon Arban. Follow the track up the stream for 3½km until you reach

Water birds to look out for here include the dipper, grey wagtail and common sandpiper.

a small sheepfold on the south side of the stream. From here take to the moor to the immediate north, then bear westwards above the horrible blanket bog that lie at the head of the Afon Arban. Climb gently up the broad ridge to the corner of a forest. Follow the forest edge westwards to the top of Crug y Wyn, and then continue around the outside of the forest to the north-west. You reach a sharp turn left in the forest fence, and should follow this over very wet ground to the south-west to the source of the Afon Tywi.

> The head of the Tywi Valley was the area where the last remaining red kites were found at the turn of the 20th century after years of persecution by man. They were at one time one of our commonest raptors, but had all but died out in Britain until this pair were found and protected by local birdwatchers. They have now spread throughout mid-Wales, and are a common sight, and many others have been successfully reintroduced to other areas of Britain.

Head south-east along the forest edge until it turns sharp right. Here you should head into the forest eastwards along a rough path until you hit a forest drive after two hundred metres. The going is hard here but it is only a very short distance. Turn right along the forest drive, ignoring the next right, and follow the track for a kilometre and a half. Where the track starts to bend towards the west, look for a track on the left that leads downhill to the bothy at Moel-prysgau. This lies right beside the Afon Tywi and is in a fine spot. Spend the night here.

Day Two: Over Drygarn Fawr

Start the day by walking downstream from the bothy and crossing the Nant Gwinau. Head around to the left and cross the Afon Tywi (this can be hard to ford in spate), picking up a public byway that leads down the valley on its eastside. Two kilometres from the ford the gurgling Nant Tadarn falls down from an open cwm to the east, and a public bridleway leads up the stream and into the forest at the top of the hill. The bridleway is not easy to follow on the ground and it is better (and much easier!) to make for a track that cuts into the forest to the south of the stream. Follow this track into the forest until you come to a clear area on the right that leads out onto the open hillside beside Afon Irfon. Cross the stream and climb over the broad ridge of Esgair yr Adar. Descend the other side over very rough ground of tussock grass and heather to the Nant y Rhestr. Here more rough tussock grass, heather and blanket bog blocks the route to the summit of **Drygarn Fawr** way over to the east. Take a bearing and stick to it, passing over the slight rise of Drum yr Eira before gaining the final summit slopes.

Two huge cairns and an OS trig pillar mark the summit of Drygarn Fawr at 641m. The name is said to come from 'three big cairns' although the whereabouts of the third is a mystery. The origins of the cairns can't be traced either. They certainly look as though they ought to be ancient, but if that were the case they would not be in such good order today.

Take a bearing south-east from the summit of Bryn Glas, then walk south over Bryn Gawr to **Banc Du**. Again this is rough country, but beyond Banc Du a bit of a path can be followed to the south-west, leading to Pen Carreg-dân at 494m. Here you will find an OS trig pillar. Just beyond the summit a fence leads down to the west to Nant Gwesyn where a public bridleway leads south-east to Trysgol. Follow the bridleway down through woods to the stream crossing, and then out through a muddy field to the lane to **Tŷ-mawr**. Turn left along the lane and out to the minor road. Turn right and walk along the road back to your car and the end of a fantastic walk.

19 – Glascwm and the Radnor Forest

Total Distance:	48km
Daily Distances:	1) 25km 2) 23km
Maps:	OS Landranger, sheet 148 *Presteigne and Hay-on-Wye, Llanandras a'r Gelli Gandryll*
Starting Point:	Glascwm village (grid ref. SO 158 533). Park sensibly by the church

Area Summary: A quiet area of low hills, this is one for the connoisseur. The Radnor Forest comprises three minor summits above 610m (2000 feet), as well as many smaller lumps and bumps on the periphery. The area is bounded to the south and west by the River Wye, to the north by the A488 running from Knighton to Llandrindod Wells, and to the east by Offa's Dyke.

Walk Summary: This is a pleasant backpacking route taking you through all kinds of scenery and over a variety of different terrain. The walk starts at Glascwm beneath the little hill of Gwaunceste before heading north for the Radnor Forest hills. You then climb onto the range at

Transport: There is no public transport to the start of this walk.

Accommodation and supplies: Best to stay in Builth Wells the night before this walk, where you can stock up on supplies and find a bed for the night. Try The Owls B&B on High Street (tel. 01982 552518) or the White Horse, also on High Street (tel. 01982 553171). Best of all is New Hall Farm B&B a mile and a half south of Builth Wells in Llanddewi'r Cwm (tel. 01982 552483).

Overnight Options: There are a couple of places to stay in New Radnor. Best to try the Eagle on Broad Street (tel. 01544 350208).

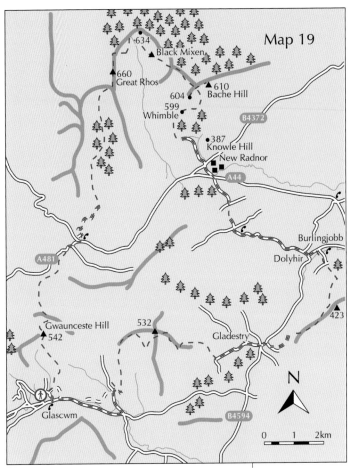

Map 19

634
▲ Black Mixen
▲660 Great Rhos
604 ● ▲ 610 Bache Hill
599 Whimble
B4372
● 387 Knowle Hill
New Radnor
A44
Burlingjobb
Dolyhir
A481
▲ 423
▲ Gwaunceste Hill
▲ 542
532 ▲
Gladestry
N
Glascwm
B4594
0   1   2km

Great Rhos and traverse the main summits before making
a way down to New Radnor for the night. On day two
you head eastwards for the Offa's Dyke Path and the fine
hill of Hergest Ridge, descending to Gladestry in time
for a pub lunch. The route then takes you westwards to
Llanfihangel Hill before heading back to Glascwm.

Day One: Gwaunceste Hill and the Radnor Forest

Start by walking eastwards through the village of **Glascwm** until the road starts to rise up the hill of Rhiw Fwnws. On the left a lane leads to the farm at Wern and you should follow this beyond the farm and down to the stream by a wood. A public bridleway leads off on the right, uphill to a col between the fine mounds of Little Hill to the south-east and Gwaunceste Hill to the north-west. Make you way over to the north-west up the long slope to the summit of **Gwaunceste Hill** at 542m. The summit is marked by an OS trig pillar.

A public bridleway passes by not far below the summit to the north-west and you should drop down to this, turning right along it to a boggy col by a tumulus where there is a junction of tracks. Take the one heading just east of north around the steep slopes of Bryn-y-maen, then onwards to a track by the shores of Llynheilyn. Bear left along the track to the main A481 road at Pool Farm. Walk to the right along the main road to a junction at Forest Inn, ignoring the minor roads on either side, passed on the way to the main road junction. Opposite the main junction a public footpath takes you across a field to Caebanol and here a track leads uphill to a

Red Grouse on
Great Rhos

narrow col between the little hills of Mynd at 479m to the south-east and Nyth-grug at 538m to the north-west. Pass straight over this col and bear round to the left along a public byway to the famous waterfalls at Water-Break-Its-Neck. ▸

The track continues up the valley above the stream and you should follow this until it is possible to nip over the stream to the right and climb up to join a track heading into a new forestry plantation. Here the main forest track takes you northwards up the ridge of Esgairnantau.

> This part of the forest is a great place to look for grasshopper warblers and tree pipits in the summer months, while it is possible that you might see a long-eared owl roosting in the trees by daylight.

Rough moorland lies ahead when you emerge from the forestry plantation, though a bit of a track can be found occasionally pointing in the right direction, and you soon find yourself squelching up the south-west flank of **Great Rhos**.

> The summit of Great Rhos, the highest hill in the Radnorshire Forest group, lies at 660m above sea level amid a sea of heather. It is marked by an OS trig pillar, which is a good job, as you would never identify the highest point on this broad plateau otherwise. The name means simply 'great moor'.

Head north by compass bearing from the summit and you will soon pick up a good track taken by a public bridleway. Turn right along this to the edge of a forest. Do not follow the track into the forest however, but turn right along the outside of the forest edge and pick up a faint path leading to the Shepherd's Well, a vague

An enthusiastic 19th-century guide used to write of this waterfall that, 'a small stream drops seventy feet into a rugged and gloomy dell amidst the wildest alpine scenery'. A bit fanciful, but the falls are definitely worth a look.

depression in the heather that is perhaps a bit more boggy than the rest of the lane hereabouts. Follow the forest edge to the south-east from the Shepherd's Well until it turn sharply to the left, and here a bit of a path leads across moorland to the summit of Black Mixen. In good weather the way is obvious as a huge mast marks the summit of **Black Mixen**.

> The summit of Black Mixen stands at 650m above sea level. There is an OS trig pillar near the mast which marks the highest point. The name comes from an old English word for a dunghill. The deep valley between Black Mixen and Great Rhos is the Harley Dingle, an area used by the MOD as a firing range.

From Black Mixen's summit you can pick up a faint path through the heather leading south-eastwards to the edge of the forest. A public bridleway skirts this as it heads southwards, and you should take this track over a little col between an un-named top to the right and Bache Hill to the left. At the top of the col you should follow a fence away from the track towards the summit of **Bache Hill**. The summit of Bache Hill lies at 610m above sea level. It's a small summit with a cairn and an OS trig pillar atop on ancient tumulus. Bache Hill means simply 'small hill'.

Head back along the fence to the bridleway to the west. Follow it downhill to the left to a large shed over another fence. Ahead to the west lies the grassy knoll of **Whimble**. A nice track climbs up this eastern ridge of the Whimble from the shed, and you should follow this to the top at 599m. ◂

Head west off the Whimble to the corner of a forest and pick up a public bridleway heading south alongside the edge of the trees. This leads downhill steeply to a road end, and you should follow this down into the village of **New Radnor** where you will spend the night.

The summit of the Whimble is a fine viewpoint for the three main hills of the Radnorshire Forest, arranged around the Harley Dingle to the north.

New Radnor is dominated by a large castle mound. This has had a turbulent history, passing from the command of the Welsh to the English and back again countless times since it was built around 1070. The village itself was in fact the county town of Radnorshire, but there is little there today other than the castle mound, a Victorian memorial to the Right Honourable Sir George Cornewall-Lewis, Baronet, and the Eagle pub.

Day Two: Hergest Ridge and Colva Hill

Walk south out of the village by the memorial and onto the main A44 road. Turn left for a short way, then right up a narrow lane that leads through pleasant woods and over the eastern ridge of the little hill known as The Smatcher. This lane takes a sharp turn left on the brow of the ridge, and here a track leads straight on down into the hamlet of Yardro. Follow this into the hamlet, ignoring lanes off to left and right until you reach the telephone box in the centre of the hamlet. Take the lane to the left by Siluria and follow it out along the northern side of the Cynon Brook to the village of **Dolyhir**, passing through some quarries along the way.

Turn left in Dolyhir onto the B4594, but after 300m take a lane on the right that takes you to Lower Hanter. Dead ahead as you walk to the farm the big lump of a mound is Hanter Hill, and you should bear right at the farm, then left immediately along a public footpath that takes you around the eastern slopes of Hanter Hill. The paths goes on and around the back of the hill to a deep col between it and Hergest Hill, and here you will pick up a public bridleway that leads steeply uphill to the south to the summit of Hergest Hill at 426m.

Hergest Hill lies on the Offa's Dyke Path national long-distance trail. Offa was King of Mercia from ▶

757 until his death in 796, Mercia being that huge Anglian kingdom which in the 6th century stretched from Wessex to Northumbria with Wales as its western border. Offa had a series of earthworks built along the Welsh border, and this national trail follows these pretty closely from Sedbury Cliffs near the Severn Bridge in the south to Prestatyn on the north coast. There is an OS trig pillar near, but not at the highest point, which lies south-west of it.

Turn to the south-west along a good track and follow the Offa's Dyke Path downhill into the lovely little village of **Gladestry**. There is a good pub here where you can get food and a drink. Turn right through the village, westwards, then right by the church on a narrow lane. Bear left at the first junction and walk uphill along the lane for 300m to another junction. Turn left again and dip to cross a stream as you make you way to Newhouse. Continue westwards to Wain Wen where the lane turns sharply left. Here, at the bend, a public bridleway crosses the stream to the right, and you should take this up onto the ridge of Cefn-hir at 511m. Continue westwards to a track that takes you up to the OS trig pillar at 532m at the summit of Colva Hill.

Leave the summit by dropping down to the west to pick up a track at Llanfihangel Hill and curve around on this track to the south-west, then to the south as you descend the steep ridge of Cnwch Bank to Cnwch Farm. Follow the driveway out of the farm onto a narrow country lane, turning left here. Follow the lane by the side of the River Arrow down to a crossroads, where you should turn right. This lane climbs steeply at first, up to the top of Rhiw Fwnws, and then takes you down into **Glascwm** and the end of this walk.

20 – The Beacons' Northern Escarpment Traverse

Total Distance:	45km
Daily Distances:	1) 24km 2) 21km
Maps:	OS Outdoor Leisure, sheet 12 *Brecon Beacons National Park West and Central Areas*
Starting Point:	The terminus of the Monmouth and Brecon Canal in Brecon, on Canal Road (grid ref. SO 046 282)
Finishing Point:	Sennibridge (grid ref. SN 921 286)

Area Summary: This is the northern escarpment of the Brecon Beacons and Fforest Fawr ranges, which lies central to the Brecon Beacons National Park in South Wales. To the north lies the River Usk, while south Wales' mining valleys lie to the south. The west of this area is bounded by the Mynydd Du range of mountains, and to the east by the Black Mountains.

Walk Summary: A grand walk over two completely different days. The walking on Day One is over good

Transport:	Brecon has good bus links with the outside world, while there are four buses daily from Sennibridge back to Brecon. Check times with the tourist information centre in the Lion Yard Car Park off Lion Street in Brecon (tel. 01874 622485)
Accommodation and supplies:	There are plenty of overnight options in Brecon, and more than enough shops too
Overnight Options:	Stay at the Llwyn-y-celyn Youth Hostel just south of Libanus (tel. 01874 624261) but book well in advance during high summer.

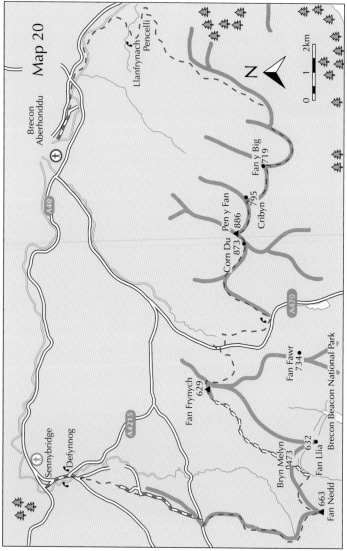

Map 20

Brecon
Aberhonddu

Llanfrynach
Pencelli

A40

Fan y Big
719

Pen y Fan
886

Corn Du
873

Cribyn
795

A470

Fan Fawr
734

Fan Frynych
629

Sennybridge
Defynnog

A4215

Brecon Beacon National Park

Bryn Melyn
1473

Fan Llia
632

Fan Nedd
663

0   1   2km

N

paths and tracks, well-trodden by all and sundry as you head east along the canal to Pencelli then gain the main ridge of the Brecon Beacons, traversing back west along the spine of the mountains before spending the night at Llwyn-y-celyn Youth Hostel. On Day Two you leave the crowds behind and head for the lonely tops of the Fforest Fawr range of hills before making a way northwards to Sennibridge where the walk ends. The walk is mainly on good tracks and paths, but with some rougher sections on Day Two.

Day One: The Brecon Beacons Main Ridge Traverse

Start this walk along the Taff Trail which runs along the south bank of the Monmouthshire and Brecon Canal. The canal is well used by narrow boats today, and the path is a popular walk for locals and tourists alike. Walk eastwards along the towpath, crossing the River Usk after 3½km. The canal crosses here by way of an aquaduct, and then continues for a further 3km to the village of Pencelli. Leave the canal via the lane on the right into the village, but turn right straight away along the lane towards **Llanfrynach**. Follow this minor road for 300m, past a junction on the

The northern escarpment

left, then on to another. Turn left here up towards Blaennant Farm. As the lane bends around towards a southerly direction, look for a public bridleway on the right, running along a good track, which leads out onto the open hillside of Clawdd Coch. The path takes you up through some fabulous scenery as you climb above the deep, wooded valley of Cwm Oergwm on your right. Soon the hillside narrows into a ridge at Bwlch Main, and the spur of Gist Wen leads onwards towards the heights of the Brecon Beacons. The route brings you out at a broad, grassy col at Rhiw Bwlch y Ddwyallt, and here you should veer off to the east to gain the first summit on the northern escarpment, Waun Rydd at 769m. The name here translates roughly as 'free moorland'.

Head back west to regain the track and follow it around the rim of the escarpment to the south-west, curving around to Bwlch y Ddwyallt. Here the escarpment edge changes direction again, and you should descend along this above Craig Cwareli at the head of Cwm Oergwm.

As you walk along this grand northern escarpment, which can actually be traced along all the four ranges of the Brecon Beacon National Park (that's the Mynydd Du, Fforest Fawr, Brecon Beacons and the Black Mountains running west to east), you can see the uniformity of the escarpment itself, and of the gradient on the gentler side of the range to the south. The rock here is from the series known as Old Red Sandstone. Each summit along this escarpment lies at the apex of the angular tip of this huge bed of slightly tilted rock, and as this bed recedes in height to the south it becomes buried beneath the carboniferous limestone which forms the famous karst scenery, pavement and potholes of the lowland hills of south Wales. Only in Scotland does the Old Red Sandstone rise to a greater height than it does here, and this combination of rock types has led to a ▶

◄ remarkable variety of plant species being able to grow in this vicinity. Nowhere further south than this will you find wild species of purple saxifrage, mossy saxifrage, roseroot or northern bedstraw, plants which really belong to the Arctic zones of the north.

Right at the very head of Cwm Oergwm the rim of the escarpment curves around to the north-west, and it is here that you'll ascend the first of the more impressive summit of this range.

Fan y Big is actually lower than Waun Rydd at just 719m, but it does have the classic Brecon Beacons mountain shape lacking in the bigger hill. Here a pointy peak juts out into the upper reaches of two cwms, separated by the long north ridge of the mountain itself. Fan y Big's name translates as 'beak beacon'.

From the summit of **Fan y Big** steep slopes drop away to the west, and you should follow the path down this way to a deep col at Bwlch ar y Fan. ►

Leave the col by climbing up steeply to the west, along the gradually curving ridge above Craig Cwm Cynwyn to the summit of **Cribyn**, another fantastic summit on the northern escarpment.

There is an old pack-horse route crossing this low col, now a busy bridleway, and some authorities will tell you that it is a Roman road.

Cribyn's name translates simple as 'the summit'. At 795m high this is a good point to obtain views of the other summits along the northern escarpment, as well as northwards across the openness of the valley of the River Usk to the distant smudges of Cwmdeuddwr Hills and even Plynlimon in the far distance. It is said that on a good day you can even see Cadair Idris from these higher Brecon Beacons, ►

◀ as well the bald, round slopes of Exmoor beyond the Bristol Channel to the south.

West again the steep slopes of the highest mountain in the Brecon Beacons, Pen y Fan, beckon. First drop down to the col between Cribyn and the main top at 665m, and then start the long climb up the ridge above Craig Cwm Sere to the lofty top of **Pen y Fan** at 886m. There is a large broken cairn and an OS trig pillar at the summit. ◀

The name translates as 'top of the beacon'. The views from here are really magnificent, covering all of south, west, and mid-Wales, and as far east as the Malverns over the English border.

An eroded path leaves the summit to the south-west and drops down to a col. A path skirts around to the south of the next summit, but you should climb straight up to its top. At 873m **Corn Du** is another fine summit, and the last main mountain of the day. Corn Du's name translates as 'black horn', which is strange given the red nature of the rock hereabouts.

Leave the summit of Corn Du to the north-west and skirt along the rim of the escarpment above Craig Cwm Llwch, descending to an Obelisk.

This obelisk commemorates the death of Tommy Jones, a young local lad who became separated from his father as they made their way over to visit relatives from Brecon Station in 1900. His body was not found for a month.

The path now heads away from the rim of the escarpment, and you should follow it to the west across moorland grasses to the low summit of Y Gyrn. Here the route turns to the south-west and a wide path leads down to the A470(T) from Brecon to Merthyr Tydfil at the Storey Arms Centre. Here on the right, just beyond the telephone box, a public bridleway, again taken by the Taff Trail, leads north into the lush, verdant valley of Glyn Tarell. Follow this public bridleway for 2km to a permissive path on the left that leads across a field to a stream. Cross this and continue out to the main road (A470(T)). Turn right and walk along the road to the youth hostel at Llwyn-y-celyn, where you will spend the night.

Day Two: Craig Cerrig-Gleisiad, Fan Frynych, and Fan Nedd

Start the day by heading out back onto the main road from the hostel. Turn left and walk along it to a parking bay and picnic area on the right. A public footpath leads up into the cwm of Craig Cerrig-gleisiad. Here you find yourself in impressive surroundings, with the cliffs themselves thrusting down upon you. This is the Craig Cerrig-gleisiad National Nature Reserve.

> The Craig Cerrig-gleisiad National Nature Reserve is a desolate cwm backed with dark buttresses and broken crags. It is famous as being one of the richest sources of alpine plants in Britain. The cwm floor is littered with boggy hollows and heathery knolls, all enclosed by a morainic mound curved around its lip. These hollows are the remnants of former cirque lakes.

At the entrance to the cwm a path leads up to the left around the top edge of the vegetated crags and you should follow this around and above the cwm itself to the summit of Craig Cerrig-gleisiad at 629m. ▸

Skirt around the rim of the cwm and down to a col, from where a path is picked up heading north-west to the next summit along the northern escarpment, Fan Frynych. The summit of **Fan Frynych**, at 629m also, is marked by an OS trig pillar. The name means 'the ox hill beacon'.

A permissive path leaves the summit of Fan Frynych to the south-west, splitting after 600m. Take the left hand track leading down beneath the escarpment. The dark, vegetated crags of Craig Cwm-du rise on your left as you walk. Soon the permissive path bends to the north-west,

A small cairn marks the top of Craig Cerrig-gleisiad, just back a little from the edge of the cwm rim. The name translates as 'blue stone rock'.

and soon after a public byway on the left should be taken at a junction.

> This byway takes the route of the old Roman road, Sarn Helen which cuts across Wales south to north. It can still be followed in many places (Sarn Helen runs north from here eventually into the Snowdonia National Park). It is believed that the Helen in question was a British wife of a Roman emperor who persuaded her husband to build this road right through Wales. However, William Condry, well-respected authority on all things historical, environmental and Welsh, in particular, claims in his book, *The Snowdonia National Park,* that ' "sarn" means a road, especially a paved road, and "elen" is a changed form of "y leng", meaning "of the legion" '. This 'road of the legion' does seem more likely to me.

Follow the track south-westwards out to a narrow lane at the top of a mountain pass after 3km. Turn right and walk along the road until you reach a permissive path on the left climbing straight up the north-east ridge of **Fan Nedd**, the large hill on your lefty as you approach. Follow this permissive path up to the short summit ridge. Turn south here and walk along the ridge to the summit of Fan Nedd. ◄

Head back north along the short summit ridge of Fan Nedd, then take to a permissive path that leads off to the north-west, dropping down to reach a wall. Follow this down to a field boundary at Bwlch y Dywynt. Hop over the wall here and follow it around to the north to the minor summit of Yr Allt at 604m. Continue alongside the boundary over rough ground to the OS trig pillar on Fan Bwlch Chwyth at 603m, continuing down to a minor lane at Penwaundwr. Turn right along this minor road for 300m to a public byway on the left. Follow this around the western side of a long, low ridge known as

Fan Nedd's summit is marked by an OS trig pillar atop a grassy mound. It lies at 663m above sea level. The name translates quite obviously as Neath Beacon.

Fforest Fawr

Waun Dŵr, eventually descending to a chapel at Clwyd-waun-dŵr at the end of another little narrow lane. Walk northwards along this lane until it turns sharply to the right, and at this point the byway continues northwards, along the fantastic ridge of Heol Cefn-y-Gaer. Follow this throughout until you come out at a lane at Glannau Senni. Turn left here and out onto the main A4067 road just outside **Defynnog**. Turn right along the main road and follow it northwards for 1km into the village of **Sennibridge**, turning left on a B road to get to the centre of the village itself.

179

21 – The Mynydd Du
and the Afon Twrch

Total Distance:	37km
Daily Distances:	1) 21km 2) 16km.
Maps:	OS Outdoor Leisure, sheet 12 *Brecon Beacons National Park West and Central Areas*
Starting Point:	The small village of Glyntawe, at the campsite for the Dan yr Ogof Caves, north of Abercraf (grid ref. SN 843 164).

Area Summary: The Mynydd Du is a fantastic area of high hills, otherwise known as the Carmarthen Vans, or Black Mountain (not to be confused with the Black Mountains east of the Brecon Beacons). The main ridge of hills lies on old red sandstone, thereby having a vast escarpment to the north. These hills fall away gradually to the south, becoming limestone and so gentler but more rocky underfoot. The range is bordered to the north by the River Usk, which finds its source just beneath the

Transport: There is a bus service from Brecon to Glyntawe (contact the tourist information office in Brecon for details, tel. 01874 622485).

Accommodation and supplies: There is a hotel and campsite at the Dan yr Ogof complex in Glyntawe where you can also arrange to leave your car whilst out on this walk (tel. 01639 730284). As there are few shops you should bring your supplies with you, or shop in Brecon (if coming from that direction) or Abercraf village (if arriving from the south).

Overnight Options: Camp wild in a delightful spot by the Afon Twrch at grid ref. SN 772 162.

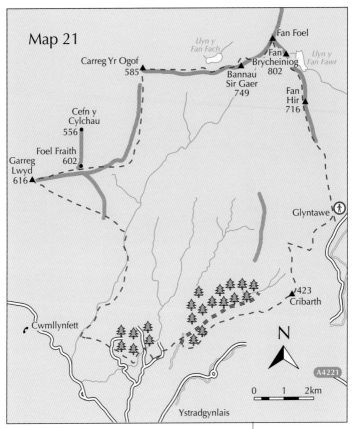

Map 21

Fan Foel

Llyn y
Fan Fach

Carreg Yr Ogof
585

Fan
Brycheiniog
802

Llyn y
Fan Fawr

Bannau
Sir Gaer
749

Fan
Hir
716

Cefn y
Cylchau
556

Foel Fraith
602

Garreg
Lwyd
616

Glyntawe

423
Cribarth

Cwmllynfett

N

A4221

0   1   2km

Ystradgynlais

northern slopes of the Mynydd Du, and to the south by the mining valleys of south Wales.

Walk Summary: A short backpacking route over some superb terrain. The going is mainly over pathless ground once the high hills have been traversed and left behind, but it is nowhere too difficult to cross nor to navigate over. On Day One you will traverse all of the high hills of the Carmarthen Vans from Glyntawe, before finding

181

Walking in the Mynydd Du

a sheltered spot to camp wild for the night by the Afon Twrch. Day Two will take you south into the valleys and forests below the limestone hills of the southern half of the range. You then follow good paths and tracks eastwards back to Glyntawe.

Day One: Over the Heights of the Mynydd Du

There is no easing into this route gently – you start climbing straight away from the campsite in **Glyntawe** and climb quickly onto the heights of the Mynydd Du. A public footpath leaves the campsite at its northern-most point and heads down to the rushing river of the Afon Haffes. Follow the stream for a short way up into Cwm Haffes, but where the fences on the right end and bring you out into open hillside, climb up to the north along a narrow spur. This takes you up onto the moor above the intake walls and you should aim northwards over the rough ground for the minor top of Allt Fach at 463m. Here you will pick up a good track leading you just west of north up the long south ridge of **Fan Hir**, the first of the main peaks of the Mynydd Du range.

Carmarthan Fan

Mynydd Du means simply 'black mountain', and should not be confused with the Black Mountains further to the east. Both ranges lie within the Brecon Beacons National Park; the Mynydd Du at the western edge of the park and the Black Mountains at the eastern. The Brecon Beacons and the Fforest Fawr ranges lie between the two. The summit of Fan Fawr is at the northern end of a long whale-back ridge. The name means 'long beacon' and has its summit marked by a small cairn at 761m above sea level.

From the top of Fan Hir a short walk to the north brings you down to a col, known as Bwlch y Giedd, and an easy climb up the other side along a good path brings you to the summit of **Fan Brycheiniog**.

At 802m Fan Brycheiniog is a fine, high mountain. It is the highest summit in the Mynydd Du range, and as such is a Mecca for walkers venturing into this area. There is a summit shelter at the top. The name translates as 'Breconshire beacon'.

Continue northwards along the rim of the steep cliffs that drop away to the east here, passing by the summit cairn at Twr y Fan Foel, also at 802m, before descending slightly to the summit of **Fan Foel** itself at 781m.

Here a path continue straight ahead, descending steeply to the north, but you should ignore this and turn to the south-west, descending along the edge of the northern escarpment that continues throughout this entire range. ◂

A deep col lies to the west of Fan Hir, Fan Brycheiniog and Fan Foel, the Bwlch Blaen-Twrch, cutting it off from the other main summit of the range. Climb westwards from the col to the summit of **Bannau Sir Gaer**, otherwise known as Picws Du, or simply Carmarthenshire Fan. The edge of the northern escarpment lies to your right as you

Old red sandstone outcrops at the main summits of the Mynydd Du range were formed by a huge tilted bed of rock, dropping gradually to the south.

climb. The summit is soon reached where an ancient cairn marks the highest point at 749m.

Continuing westwards the path becomes less well-defined, although it is still fairly obvious. Skirt the edge of the escarpment down to another little col after 1½km. This lies above a steep and very loose gully coming up from the shores of Llyn y Fan Fach at the bottom of the escarpment.

There is an ancient and over told story about this lake and of the mother of the Physicians of Myddfai. She is said to have come from out of Llyn y Fan Fach and after being beaten three times by her husband decided enough was enough and went back into its murky waters. She was only seen once more, by her three sons upon whom she bestowed the knowledge that would make them great men of medicine.

Continue along the rim from the top of the gully, bearing north-west for the broad, featureless summit of Waun Lefrith at 677m. From here you leave the edge of the escarpment behind and take a compass bearing westwards for the OS trig pillar at 585m on **Carreg yr Ogof** (grid ref. SO 777 215). This lies just over 2km away to the west, and the route takes you on an easy descent over grass and bilberry to a broad col, then uphill over rough limestone crags to the top.

Head south from the summit of Carreg yr Ogof, down to a col, then up the stony north ridge of Garreg Las to its fine summit cairn amid layers of limestone pavement.

The summit of Garreg Las is a fine place, one of my favourite Welsh summits in fact, and at 635m you have a wonderful view of the southern slopes of the main ridge of the Mynydd Du. Garreg Las translates as 'blue stone', which is a good name for a hill showing so much limestone around its top.

Crossing the Mynydd Du

Turn and follow the ridge southwards, keeping to the right-hand side which gives pleasant walking on rough limestone pavement to the flat plateau of Godre r Garreg Las. From here turn your back on Garreg Las and descend rough ground to the south-west, making your way towards the lonely little pool of Blaenllynfell on a boggy col. Continue westwards from here, climbing the rocky slopes of **Foel Fraith** to its summit at 602m, then onwards to the west down to another col. Ahead lies the last summit of the day, **Garreg Lwyd** and easy slopes covered with moorland grasses and limestone scree lead up to its huge and ancient cairn at 616m.

From the top of Garreg Lwyd you should drop down into the headwaters of the River Amman, but do not drop down to far into the valley. Instead, contour around the head of the cwm to Cefn Carn Fadog, and climb easily up to its little summit at 507m with a lonely moorland tarn nearby. Walking on a bearing for 1km to the south-east will lead you down off the hills to a fine camping spot by the Afon Twrch, where the springs of Ffrydiau Twrch rise off the side of Cefn Carn Fadog.

Pitch your tent here and bed down for the night in this lovely valley.

Day Two: The Afon Twrch and Nany Cyw

On the east side of the Afon Twrch a public footpath comes up out of the valleys and crosses the stream at the point where you camped last night. Cross over to the east side and follow this path downstream. It is easy to follow as it makes its way down to a crossing of a little stream on the left below a waterfall, then on to the farmstead at Dorwen. Beyond this the public right of way heads down to the banks of the river again, but the easiest way to follow on the ground is to continue along the main track which climbs back up onto the moor beneath some standing stones and an ancient cairn, then follow this track south-westwards down a ridge to Waun-lwyd and a minor road. Turn left along this minor road to where it ends and becomes a public byway. Continue along this byway, entering a forest as you climb gently.

Go straight ahead at a junction of tracks upon entering the forest, then continue to the south-east at all other junctions, passing a large pool on your left and dropping down to a bridge over the Nant Gwys at Tîr-y-gôf-Bridge. Do not cross the river here, but instead continue on a track along its northern bank, through the forest to Bryngrunin and another bridge. Cross over here to the farm at Bryngrunin and follow a public footpath over a low rise and down to a footbridge over a little stream. Climb up the other side to a narrow lane at Hen-glyn-isaf. Turn left and follow the lane eastwards, continuing around a sharp bend left after 400m. Two hundred metres after the bend a public footpath sign on the right points along the outside of a series of fields, then drops down through a fine woodland to a bridge over the confluence of the Afon Giedd and the Nant Cyw.

Cross the rivers and turn right along a path, heading downstream for 300m until it climbs away from the river and up to a minor road. Head eastwards along this road to Neudd-lŵyd, then continue around a bend to

187

The Afon Giedd is actually wrongly named. Follow it with the eye on the map and it looks as though if you were to walk along its course to its source you would head straight into the Mynydd Du mountains to where it rises to the west of the little summit of Disgwlfa. Continuing in the same direction you come to a pothole, or sink, known as Sinc y Giedd before continuing to its source high up at Bwlch y Giedd between Fan Hir and Fan Brycheiniog. This is not the case however. The stream that sinks at Sinc y Giedd actually rises again at the Dan yr Ogof caves where you started this walk. This cave system lies 3⅙km to the east of the sink, and so must take a very sharp turn left after vanishing underground. This had fooled cartographers from the Ordnance Survey for years, until potholers put coloured dye into the sink to see where it would emerge during the early exploration of the cave systems that abound in these hills.

the north-east and onto a public byway. This skirts the southern side of a forest before becoming a public footpath, and you should follow this around field edges to emerge onto open moorland below Cribarth. The path continues climbing to the north-east to the summit of **Cribarth** at 426m. Take a compass bearing to the corner of a fence 800m away to the north and follow this. The fence heads north towards Carreg a'r Gap, then turns to the east. Follow this all the way around and drop to the huge sinkhole of Pwll-yr-Cawr. Continue along the uphill side of the fence to the north-east until you pick up a public bridleway that leads down to the Dan yr Ogof cave complex and the end of a fine walk.

22 – The Fforest Fawr Range
From Ystradfellte

Total Distance:	39km
Daily Distances:	1) 24km 2) 15km
Maps:	OS Outdoor Leisure, sheet 12 *Brecon Beacons National Park West and Central Areas*
Starting Point:	The fine little mountain village of Ystradfellte, in the middle of the Fforest Fawr range (grid ref. SN 930 134).

Area Summary: A wild, remote-feeling wilderness of tussock grass hills and heather, the Fforest Fawr has never been popular as a mountain range. This is probably due to its proximity to much greater things, such as the Brecon Beacons and the Black Mountains. However, the walking here is fine, and you are unlikely to feel crowded in these lonely hills. The range has the Brecon Beacon massif immediately to the east and the Mynydd Du (Black Mountain) range to the west.

Transport:	There is no regular public transport service to the start of this walk
Accommodation and supplies:	There is not much in Ystradfellte other than a popular walker's pub, the New Inn, a youth hostel just down the road (tel. 01639 720301) and the campsite at Pennllwyn-Einon Farm Bungalow (tel. 01639 720542). It is best to bring your supplies with you for this walk.
Overnight Options:	Book well in advance to use the youth hostel at Llwyn-y-celyn (tel. 01874 624261) just south of Libanus (grid ref. SN 974 225).

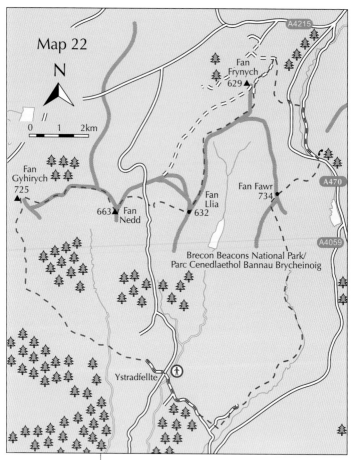

Map 22

N

0 1 2km

Fan
Frynych
629 ▲

Fan
Gyhirych
725 ▲

663 ▲ Fan
Nedd

Fan
Llia
632 ●

Fan Fawr
734 ●

A4215

A470

A4059

Brecon Beacons National Park/
Parc Cenedlaethol Bannau Brycheiniog

Ystradfellte

Walk Summary: A fine walk over little-used paths and
tracks with occasional forays onto rougher stuff. The
walk starts with a fantastic system of footpaths leading
north-west for the open hillside of Fan Gyhirych, the
most westerly peak of the range, then brings you back
to the east across the hills to the youth hostel at Libanus

for the night. On Day Two you will follow the Taff Trail for a short way southwards before climbing Fan Fawr, possibly the only popular hill of the range due to its ease of access from the Storey Arms. You will then follow streams southwards back to Ystradfellte.

Day One: Fan Gyhirych to Fan Frynych

From the post office in **Ystradfellte** a little dead-end lane leads westwards and becomes a track at a crossroads. Go straight ahead along the track, now a public byway, and out onto the open hillside. The byway turns to the north-west, while a public bridleway heads west uphill to an iron-age hill fort before dropping gradually to a narrow lane just south of Blaen-nedd-Isaf. Turn right along the lane to the farm, dropping down to cross the lovely river of the Nedd Fechan at a footbridge. Climb up beside a little wood, then up to a junction of paths at the corner of a Forestry Commission plantation. From the junction a public footpath heads off to the north-west across open rough grassland and moorland. Continue for 2km to a field boundary, then follow the edge of this until it is possible to head northwards to the little summit of Carn yr Onnen at 524m.

Head north alongside the boundary, bearing north-west across the headwaters of the Byfre Fechan to a track that leads up to the south side of Fan Gyhirych. This bulldozed track leads up towards the summit, but veers away to the east before taking you up to the summit itself. A little path leads off through the heather to the left, bringing you to the summit of Fan **Gyhirych**.

The translation of Fan Gyhirych is unknown. Its top is marked by an OS trig pillar, and a short walk to the north from the summit gives a great view point for the whole of the Usk valley and beyond to the hills of Mid Wales. The summit is 725m high.

Fan Gyhirych, Fforest Fawr

The summit of Fan Nedd is marked by an OS trig pillar at 663m above sea level. The name means 'Neath beacon'.

Just north of the point where the path reaches the road lies Maen Llia, a standing stone marking the top of this ancient packhorse route and drovers trail.

Return to the bulldozed track and head eastwards along it for 200m, until the north ridge of Fan Fraith leads up to the right. This little summit gives a short diversion, and although you will have to return to the main track you should head up to its top at 668m.

Return once again to the bulldozed track and follow it to the north-east to a gate. A permissive footpath leads downhill on the right to col above the headwaters of the Blaen Senni. The permissive path leads up the north-west ridge of Fan Nedd, and you should climb up this gradually to the northern tip of the short summit ridge. Turn to the south and follow the ridge to the summit of **Fan Nedd**. ◄

Head back north along the short ridge to the place where you climbed up from the north-west. Here the permissive path takes you off down the north-east ridge to a minor road at the head of a pass. ◄

Turn right for a short way along the road, and then pick up a public byway, a good track on the ground, heading north-east.

This byway takes the route of the old Roman road, Sarn Helen, which cuts across Wales south to ►

⁌ north (Sarn Helen runs north from here, eventually into the Snowdonia National Park). It can still be followed in many places. Although it is believed that the Helen in question was a British wife of a Roman emperor who persuaded her husband to build this road right through Wales, William Condry, a well-respected authority on all things Welsh claims in his book, *The Snowdonia National Park,* that, '"sarn" means a road, especially a paved road, and "elen" is a changed form of "y leng", meaning "of the legion"'. This 'road of the legion' seems more likely to me.

Walk along Sarn Helen for 500m, until the river on the right can be crossed easily. The long whale-backed ridge of Fan Llia rises to the east and you should leave the track and make for this ridge. Bear right once on the ridge and walk to the summit of **Fan Llia**. ⁍

Leave the summit of Fan Llia and walk northwards along the ridge, descending slightly to the minor top of Fan Dringarth, then on along the long grassy ridge of Cefn Perfedd to the rim of the northern escarpment of the Brecon Beacons National Park at Craig Cwm-du.

Fan Llia, or 'Llia's beacon' is 632m high, and is good place to view Fan Fawr to the east and Fan Nedd to the west.

This northern escarpment is the point where the underlying rock, the old red sandstone, tilts to its apex. The bed of rock falls gradually away to the south.

Turn to the east and drop down to a broad, featureless col, then on upwards towards the distant summit of Craig Cerrig-gleisiad. ⁍

Follow the rim of the cliffs around to the north, dropping to a col, then up to the summit of **Fan Frynych**, set back from the cliffs slightly at 629m.

A permissive footpath leads down off Fan Frynych to the north-east, along the grand ridge of Twyn Dylluan-ddu. At a path junction beside a stand of fine pine trees,

The summit lies close to the edge of the cliffs of the Craig Cerrig-gleisiad National Nature Reserve. Many rare plants can be found here.

a public footpath leads back underneath the cliffs of the Nature Reserve, and you should follow this around the base of the cwm. Keep above the intake wall until a path leads out to the main road and a picnic site at a lay-by. Turn left along the main road (the A470(T)), until the entrance to the youth hostel at Llwyn-y-celyn is reached on the right after 400m. Turn right down the driveway and spend the night here.

Day Two: Fan Fawr and the Afon y Waun

Start the day by heading out onto the main road from the hostel. Turn left and walk on past the lay-by to a permissive footpath on the left which leads down to a little stream where a footbridge leads over and up to a public bridleway above. This bridleway is taken by the Taff Trail, and you should turn right and follow this gently uphill to the head of the Afon Tarell where the trail meets the main road at the Storey Arms Outdoor Centre.

Here there is a car park on the other side of the road, and from here a footpath leads up above the moorlands of Bryn Du to the north-east ridge of **Fan Fawr**. The path is well-worn and obvious, and soon leads you to the ridge itself which curves around to the left, keeping the steep drop of Cefn Bach on your left. The summit lies a little way back from the edge.

Leave the summit of Fan Fawr and walk to the south-west to the prominent OS trig pillar at 715m. Ahead lies much rough ground, but the walk is all downhill from here, and takes you into the delightfully wild valley of the Afon y Waun.

> The name Fan Fawr means simply 'big beacon', and a cairn at 734m marks its summit. There is an OS trig pillar 800m further on, but this is not the highest point. However, this walk heads over that way to a fine viewpoint overlooking the valley of Afon Dringarth holding the Ystradfellte Reservoir.

Waterfall near
Ystradfellte

Take a bearing to the south, heading downhill into the headwaters of the Afon y Waun. Stay on the west side of the river, following it downstream to the summer pastures of Hepste-fechan just above the main river, where a footbridge leads over the side stream of the Nant Hepste-fechan. A public footpath now takes you onwards, still on the true right bank of the Afon y Waun and down to the end of a public road at Llwyn-y-fedwen. Walk down the road, passing Hepste-fawr and on to the small conifer plantation of Gweunydd Hepste on the right. Turn left with the road, then where it bears right a public footpath leads off on the right through the forest to Pwll-y Felin, a large limestone swallow hole. Here you join another minor road and you should turn right along this for 300m, bearing left at the junction and continuing along the lane for just over 1km to another road junction. Turn right here and walk down into the village of **Ystradfellte** where you end this fantastic walk.

23 – The Brecon Beacons

Total Distance:	40km
Daily Distances:	1) 26km 2) 14km
Maps:	OS Outdoor Leisure, sheet 12 *Brecon Beacons National Park West and Central Areas* and sheet 13, *Brecon Beacons National Park Eastern Area*
Starting Point:	The fine little mountain village of Pontsticill, in a lay-by beneath the dam of the Pontsticill Reservoir (grid ref. SO 059 115).

Area Summary: The Brecon Beacons is a fantastic mountain range, arguably the most important for the walker in south Wales. The range itself lies central to the Brecon Beacons National Park. To the north lies the River Usk, while the south Wales mining valleys lie to the south. The west of this mountain group is bounded by the Fforest Fawr range of hills, and to the east rise the Black Mountains.

Walk Summary: A grand walk taking in good paths, well-trodden by all and sundry, along the main ridge of the

Transport: There is no public transport to Pontsticill

Accommodation and supplies: There's nothing much in Talybont, but some B&Bs in Merthyr Tydfil and Cefn-coed-y-cymmer just to the south-west. There is a good campsite at Grawen Farm (tel. 01685 723740) in Llwyn-on village west of Pontsticill on the road to Brecon heading north from Merthyr Tydfil (grid ref. SO 015 111).

Overnight Options: Camp at Pencelli Castle Camping and Caravan Site (tel. 01874 665451)

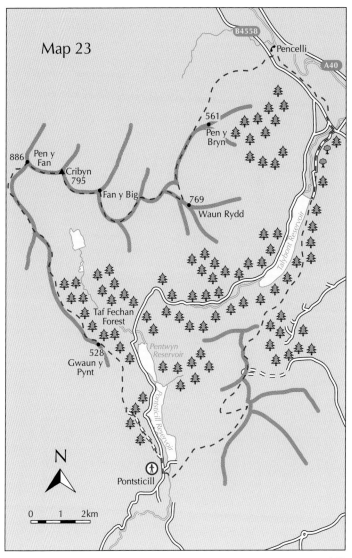

Map 23

Brecon Beacons, traversing east along the spine of the mountains on the first day before spending the night at Pencelli at the campsite there. On Day Two you follow the Taff Trail southwards to Talybont Reservoir, from where good woodland tracks lead you up onto the outlying hill of Cefn yr Ystrad before heading back to Pontsticill.

Day One: The High Summits of the Brecon Beacons

Walk westwards uphill from the small parking area beneath the dam in **Pontsticill**, up into the village itself, the turn right along the high street. Walk northwards along this road until you leave the village behind and enter a forest just beyond a car park on the right. At this point a public footpath, taken by the Taff Trail, heads gently uphill on the left into the forest. ◄

These big conifer plantations are great places for bird watching. Coal tits, goldcrests, siskins and even crossbills can often be seen feeding in the tree tops.

Follow the track through the wood for 2½km to a point where it turns sharply towards the south-east as you cross a stream. Open hillsides rise to your left and you should leave the forest here and pick up a path alongside a small enclosure. The path leads uphill to the broad-shouldered slopes of **Gwaun y Pynt** at 528m. Here you reach the top edge of the forest again, and you should keep above it, walking parallel to it as you head north-west for 3km to an OS trig pillar at 642m.

Just beyond this OS trig pillar the valley opens up to your right and the views across to the main tops of the Brecon Beacons are superb. Below lie the dark, rhododendron-edged waters of the Neuadd Reservoirs, while at the head of the valley the flat-topped summits of Corn Du, Pen y Fan and Cribyn fill the view.

Skirt around the upper edge of the broken crags to your right as you walk up the ridge of Graig Fan Ddu and on to a little cairn on the minor summit of Cefn Cul.

Ahead the ridge narrows at Rhiw yr Ysgyfarnog and the path handrails along this.

The head of the Blaen Taf Fechan can still be seen to your right, but here on the narrow ridge the views into lonely Cwm Crew on the left are impressive. Swallows and house martins follow this ridge in summer, skimming along on the uplift from the two valleys, while peregrines nest on the crags beneath.

Beyond the narrows on Rhiw yr Ysgyfarnog the path leads up to another minor summit atop Craig Gwaun Taf, then curves around the rim to the right and down to an eroded col. Straight ahead the little rise takes you up the south-west ridge of Corn Du, and you should follow the path to this great summit. ▶

The path drops to the north-east, down to a high col between Corn Du and Pen y Fan, the highest mountain in the Brecon Beacons. Head down this ridge, then up the other side to the large summit cairn atop **Pen y Fan**.

The summit of Corn Du is at 873m above sea level. The names translates as the 'black horn', which is odd as all the exposed rock around here is fine old red sandstone.

The views on a good day take your eye as far as Cadair Idris from the summit of Pen y Fan, as well as to the bald, rounded slopes of Exmoor beyond the Bristol Channel to the south, and as far east as the Malverns over the English border. The summit of Pen y Fan is at 886m. The name means 'top of the beacon'.

From the summit of Pen y Fan a ridge drops away steeply to the south-east, and you should follow this along a good, though eroded path, skirting above Craig Cwm Sere and down to a low col at 665m. The path continues from this col by taking you up the even steeper west ridge of the next big mountain along this humped-

The name Cribyn translates as 'the summit', which is fair given the impressive, classical pointy mountain shape of the peak.

Beak beacon, to give a direct translation of Fan y Big, is another fine top. Its summit lies at 719m and has a good wind shelter at the highest point in which you can sit to admire the views.

back chain, **Cribyn**. The way is obvious and you soon find yourself at the summit at 795m. ◄

Cribyn's summit lies at the meeting point of two wild cwms; Cwm Sere is to the north-west and Cwm Cynwyn to the north-east. The path now drops around the head of the latter cwm, skirting the top edge of Craig Cwm Cynwyn to the south-east as you descend to another low col, this one crossed by an ancient pack horse route. From this col at 599m, known as Bwlch ar y Fan, a short climb eastwards leads up over short-cropped grass where Black Mountain ponies graze, to the summit of **Fan y Big**. ◄

A long ridge runs south from the summit of Fan y Big, and the path follows this around to the head of the next big cwm to the east, Cwm Oergwm. Walk around the rim of this, handrailing to a col at Craig Cwmoergwm, then skirt over to the east up to the broad plateau of Gwaun Gerrig Llwydion. Stay close by the edge of the northern escarpment here, following the path over to Bwlch y Ddwyallt and on to a narrow col at the head of Blaen y Glyn which falls steeply to the south. This col is also marked on the map as Bwlch y Ddwyallt. From here grassy slopes draw you away from the rim of the escarpment towards the summit of **Waun Rydd**, and you should

Brecon Beacons

head up here on what is a minor detour to the small summit cairn at 769m. The cairn lies to the left of the path on the top of the first rise.

Return to the public footpath to the west at the edge of the northern escarpment and turn to the north-east, following the path down the long ridge of Gist Wen. ›

Follow the path down the ridge, keeping to the left of **Pen y Bryn** and on down the lower flanks to a minor road just outside Pencelli. Turn left along the lane and follow it downhill to a T-junction. Turn right here and walk into the village of **Pencelli**. The campsite is through the village along the main road heading eastwards.

The ridge of Gist Wen separates the wild cwms of Cwm Oergwm and Cwm Banw, giving fine views into both as you descend.

Day Two: Along the Taff Trail to Cefn Yr Ystrad

Walk back along the road into the village to where it cuts over the Monmouthshire and Brecon Canal at a bridge. Cross the bridge and take to the towpath on the right, heading eastwards along this. Follow the towpath for 3½km to Talybont-on-Usk. Cross over the Caerfanell river and bear right up a bridleway to cross over an old disused railway. Turn right along a bridleway, signposted as the Taff Trail, and follow this around the lower slopes of a tree-covered hill to your left. The bridleway skirts the bottom of the wood, and after just over 1km the track splits. Take the right-hand track down to the dam of the **Talybont Reservoir**. Here the tracks split again as you come to the bed of the disused railway. The Taff Trail follows the line of the old railway, whereas down on the right, running parallel to this, is a public bridleway. Follow this bridleway as it drops right down to the shores of Talybont Reservoir. ›

Just over 1km from the track junction, the public bridleway starts to head uphill and passes underneath the old railway line and the Taff Trail. Follow this uphill, continuing as it climbs up through coniferous woodland to eventually emerge at Pen Rhiw-calch. Ignore the track that heads back down into the forest and walk out to the open hillside. Just south-west of Pen Rhiw-calch the bridleway splits again at a junction, and you should take

This is a good place to look for breeding common sandpipers in the summer months, while in winter the reservoir is a great spot for goldeneye, goosander and red-breasted merganser ducks.

Resting on
Cefn Yr ystrad

the one on the right, now a public byway, that passes
beneath a series of little knolls at Pen Bwlch Glasgwm
and goes on to another track junction just beyond a col.
Take the left-hand track, crossing rough moorland and
climbing gradually to the horrible open quarries of Cwar
yr Ystrad. Follow the track through the quarries to the
south-west until you come out onto the open hillside
again. Here turn left uphill over pathless terrain to the
large summit cairns and OS trig pillar of Cefn yr Ystrad
at 617m.

Take a compass bearing to the south-west, making
for a cluster of little pools in the limestone plateau at
Twynau Gwynion, then head down the rough slopes
to the west to pick up a public bridleway at a junction.
Take the track going downhill to the top of an enclosed
wood, then across pleasant flower meadows to a tunnel
leading underneath the Brecon Mountain Railway. The
bridleway continues downhill to a public road across the
valley from Pontsticill, and at this point on the road a
junction takes you off down the hill straight ahead to the
west to your car at the bottom of the Pontsticill dam.

24 – Black Mountains from Crickhowell

Total Distance:	48km
Daily Distances:	1) 31km 2) 17km
Maps:	OS Outdoor Leisure, sheet 13 *Brecon Beacons National Park Eastern Area*
Starting Point:	The fine market town of Crickhowell at the foot of the Black Mountains (grid ref. SO 217 185)

Area Summary: These are hard hills to cross, not in the rocky sense, but in the boggy sense. The Black Mountains have long-since had a reputation as being akin to the likes of Kinder Scout in the Peak District, or Yockenthwaite Moor in Yorkshire – they are very wet hills indeed. You have been warned! The area is bounded to the north by the River Wye as it flows through Hay-on-Wye, to the south by the River Usk as it flows through Crickhowell, to the east by the border with England (in fact the border actually runs along the ridge of Black Mountain itself), and to the west by the Brecon Beacons.

Transport: There are hourly buses to Crickhowell from Abergavenny, which is on the train line from Cardiff

Accommodation and supplies: There is no shortage of B&B accommodation in Crickhowell, and you should call in at the Tourist Information Centre on Beaufort Street for ideas (tel. 01837 812105). There is a good campsite down by the river at Riverside Park (tel. 01873 810397). You can buy all your supplies in Crickhowell, including walking gear.

Overnight Options: Use the Mountain Bothy Association bothy at Grwyne Fawr Reservoir, a little stone hut at the northern end (grid ref. SO 226 312).

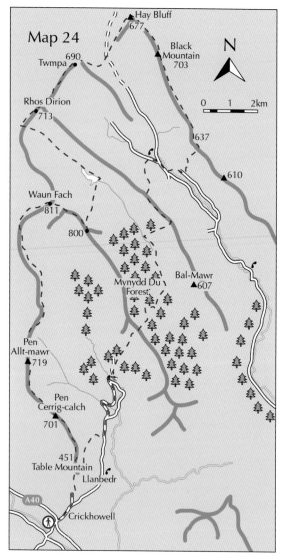

Map 24

Hay Bluff
677

Black
Mountain
703

Twmpa
690

N

Rhos Dirion
713

0   1   2km

637

610

Waun Fach
811

800

Bal-Mawr
607

Mynydd Du
Forest

Pen
Allt-mawr
719

Pen
Cerrig-calch
701

451
Table Mountain
Llanbedr

A40

Crickhowell

Walk Summary: A great walk for those who love bog-trotting. This is a strenuous route, taking in all the principal summits of the Black Mountains range. The walk does follow paths for most of its length, but sometimes it is actually easier to ignore them and cross the open moorland instead. On Day One you'll leave Crickhowell in the direction of Table Mountain, skirting around its base to the east and making for the lovely valley of the Grwyne Fechan. The route crosses forested ridges as it makes for Chwarel y Fan, a low hill on the edge of the Vale of Ewyas. You then drop down into the Vale before climbing Black Mountain to the east. This leads on a long ridge around to the west, then south to the lonely bothy at Grwyne Fawr Reservoir for the night. You start the day by climbing the top main peaks of the Black Mountains range, Pen y Gadair Fawr and Waun Fach. The route then takes you onto slightly easier hills as you traverse over to Pen Cerrig-calch. A gentle walk leads down over Table Mountain back to Crickhowell.

Day One: Across the Grain of the Black Mountains

Walk westwards along the A40(T) from the market place in **Crickhowell** until you come to the first junction on

The Black Mountains

the right. Follow this lane uphill to a road junction at the Great Oak and turn left here, walking around the bend for 200m. On the left a public bridleway leads uphill along field edges to the farm called The Wern. Bear right at the farm, along a public footpath, then left at the next field boundary. The footpath follows a lane uphill to an old stand of pines at a farm, then runs eastwards around the lower slopes of Crug Hywell, or **Table Mountain** as it is invariably known.

> The story goes that Hywell Dda, or Hywell the Good, was the grandson of the great Welsh King Rhodri in the ninth century. His fort on the flat-topped hill (hence Table Mountain) was the first settlement in this area. The town of Crickhowell obviously takes its name from this, 'crug' meaning 'mount'.

The public footpath leads to a junction, where all interesting paths seem to head for the summit of Crug Hywell. Resist the temptation however. You will have ample time to explore the fort tomorrow on your return to Crickhowell. At the junction go straight ahead, northwards along the top side of the intake wall, veering to the north-east as it descends slightly. Continue along the wall until you reach another path coming up on the right from Graig-lwyd.

Turn right and follow this path downhill to the minor road below the cottage. Turn left along the lane and follow it northwards for 800m to a junction. Take the left turn and continue along the lane, around a big bend to the right, then another bend to the left below Neuadd-fawr farm. Stay on the road, passing Pentwyn and walk on to another junction where you turn sharp right. One hundred metres down this lane on the left there is a public footpath which follows a stream then veers off to the right and up through a wood to a track. Here you emerge from beneath the trees and turn sharp left along the footpath, looking for a gate on the right where the path takes you away from the forest edge and uphill above Nantyrychain Farm.

Continue climbing diagonally up the hillside to re-enter the forest for a short distance, then continue onto the open hill in a steep-sided cwm. The path climbs to the south-east of the Nant yr Ychen, the stream that has formed the cwm, then leads up to the ridge above at a col by a cairn. Cross straight over the ridge and drop down into the dark forests on the other side, following the footpath to the north-east into the trees and veering around to the head of Cwm Ddeunant. Continue down the north side of the stream, turning left at a junction of tracks, then sharp right at a point where more tracks cross. Follow this downhill all the way to a minor road in the deep valley of the Grwyne Fawr, just south of Nantybedd. Turn left along the lane, passing Nantybedd and walking on around a left bend. Just beyond the bend there is a footbridge on the right that takes you over the Grwyne Fawr. Cross over the stream here and turn left upstream along a public byway. Follow this for 1½km to a car park. Take the right-hand track beyond the car park, walking to the north-west to a junction of tracks in the forest. Turn right here and climb directly uphill to the top right-hand corner of the forest, immediately below the summit of Chwarel y Fan. A little stream tumbles down from near the summit and you can climb alongside this to a felled area of trees. The summit lies directly above. ▸

Leave the summit by turning left along the ridge, walking north-westwards down to a large cairn and standing stone, known as the Blacksmith's Arms. Here a public bridleway crosses the ridge and turning right down this you should walk northwards down to the minor lane in the tiny hamlet of Capel y Ffin. Turn right along the lane to a junction, where you should turn right again. Walk down the lane for 1km to a track on the left taken by a public footpath. This leads down to a footbridge over the Afon Honddu, then up through fields to The Vision Farm. On the left hand side of the farm buildings there is a public footpath that leads up through a little wood and out onto the open hillside above the farm

The summit lies atop a fine little ridge at 679m above sea level. The name Chwarel y Fan translates as 'quarry beacon'.

and Nant Vision. This path zigzags in broad sweeps onto the high ridge of Black Mountain at a pile of stones. ◄

Turn left along the border ridge, picking up the tracks of Offa's Dyke walkers as you head north-west towards distant Black Mountain.

Here you find yourself on the boundary between Wales and England, and as you walk along the ridge it is possible to have a leg in either, although you would never know it on the ground!

Offa was King of Mercia from 757 until his death in 796, Mercia being that huge Anglian kingdom which in the 6th century stretched from Wessex to Northumbria with Wales on its western border. Offa had a series of earthworks built along the Welsh border, and the Offa's Dyke national trail follows these pretty closely from Sedbury Cliffs near the Severn Bridge in the south to Prestatyn on the north coast.

The route climbs gently for 3½km to the unassuming summit of **Black Mountain** at 703m high. ◄

Continue along the eroded path northwards, dropping down to a col after nearly 2km, then up the other side to the summit of **Hay Bluff**.

The actual summit of Black Mountain is difficult to find and is not marked by a cairn or trig pillar.

Hay Bluff gives a fantastic viewpoint over the River Wye to the north. Immediately beneath the hill's flanks is the 'Book Town' of Hay-on-Wye. An OS trig pillar at 677m marks the summit.

From the top of Hay Bluff a track leads off to the south-west along a gradually descending ridge known as Ffynnon y Parc. Follow this down to the minor road at Gospel Pass at 538m. Cross over the road and head slightly left to a path that climbs up an eroded gully. Follow this up the edge of a ridge above to the summit of **Twmpa**, or Lord Hereford's Knob, at 690m high. A cairn marks the summit. Head off to the south-west keeping the rim of the escarpment to your left. The path leads over grassy ground to a col, then onwards up the broad north-east ridge of **Rhos Dirion** at 713m. Continue to the south-west down to the next col where a public byway is reached. This crosses the range from the north to run down into the Grwyne Fawr valley. Turn left along this track and follow it down into the valley, walking for just over 2km to the head of the Grwyne Fawr Reservoir where you will find the small bothy in which you can spend the night.

Day Two: Waun Fach and Pen Allt-Mawr

Start the day by walking along the public byway to the south-east, contouring above the northern shore of the Grwyne Fawr Reservoir. At the dam you can cross over to the south-east corner and here you should leave the track and begin the long climb southwards towards the summit of Pen y Gadair Fawr. The going here is hard, but a steady pace will soon have at the large cairn which marks the summit at 800m. The name Pen y Gadair Fawr translates as 'head of the great chair'.

Here a vague path leaves the summit and takes you towards the north-west. Follow this down to a broad col, often very boggy, then curve around to the left slightly and cross wet, marshy ground to the summit of **Waun Fach**.

The summit of Waun Fach is the highest in the Black Mountains at 810m. It is also one of the boggiest tops you will find anywhere. The name translates as 'little moor', which is surprising to say the least. The summit itself is marked by an OS trig pillar, although it is usually impossible to reach this without getting very wet and muddy as it lies within a broad circle of oozing peat that is deep enough to make me not want to tread on it! Beware.

Take a compass bearing from the summit of Waun Fach and follow it westwards down to a narrowing ridge. This is still very boggy, but as you leave the little plateau of the summit a path emerges underfoot and at least makes navigation easier, even if the walking is still hard. The ridge continues and narrows further at Pen Trumau, then takes a swing to the south as you near a steep-sided col by a cairn. Climb up the ridge to the south of the col, reaching the little summit of Mynydd Llysiau at 663m.

The summit of Mynydd Llysiau is a fine viewpoint. From the little cairn you can look deep into the head of the Grwyne Fechan valley to the east and across the deep trench of the Afon Rhiangoll to the fine hills of Mynydd Troed and Mynydd Llangorse to the west.

Follow the ridge to the south-east from the summit, dropping down to a high col at 623m. Continue southwards to the boundary stone-marked summit of Pen Twyn Glas at 646m, then head off westwards to pick up a path down to a grassy col. The path veers off to the south-west, towards the steep and imposing north ridge of **Pen Allt-mawr**. Follow this up the ridge to the superb summit cairn and viewpoint.

At 719m the summit of Pen Allt-mawr is a great place to take in the fine ridges of the Black Mountains and Brecon Beacons. Many of the smaller hills of these two ranges look dramatic from here too. To the north-west Mynydd Troed and Mynydd Llangorse still look superb, while to the east Sugar Loaf rises high above Abergavenny. The name Pen Allt-mawr means 'big hill end', and as well as a huge cairn built from millstone grit blocks there is an OS trig pillar.

Two paths leave the summit of Pen Allt-mawr towards the south. They both skirts edge of the flat plateau, and you should take care to follow the one to the south-east, keeping along the rim of the huge drop into Cwm Banw to the east.

The edges of these plateau are a great place to see swallows and house martins in the summer. They use the rising thermals to zip along at high speed in pursuit of insects. Peregrine falcons also sometimes nest on these mountains crags.

The path is obvious though often wet and peaty. It leads down to a col beside a cairn, then up easy slopes to the impressive boulder-field top of **Pen Cerrig-calch** at 701m.

Pen Cerrig-calch's summit is aptly named. It translates as 'limestone head'. This is the only hill in the Black Mountains range to be capped by carboniferous limestone, hence the vast scattering of fine white blocks near the ancient summit cairn and OS trig pillar. For those with an interest in wildflowers, there is a wide range to look out for near the summit. Bilberry, cowberry, cloudberry, crowberry and tormentil can be seen everywhere, while there are ling, bell and cross-leaved heathers too. The wetter parts of the plateau hold round and oval-leaved sundews, as well as butterwort, lousewort and milkwort.

The path continues to the south-east and you should follow this to the edge of the plateau. Below lies the little flat-topped hill of Crug Hywel. Drop down steeply on the path, taking a big zigzag over to the left. This leads you

Pen Cerrig-calch

The top here has a good sprinkling of gorse bushes dotted around its slopes, as well as some small birch trees. Walkers with an interest in wildlife should look for willow warblers, stonechats and whinchats here during the summer months.

down to a stony col before the gentle rise to the summit of Crug Hywel. ◄

Return to the col and bear left off the edge of Crug Hywel. A path leads back beneath the little hill on its western slopes, and then takes you down to The Wern on the series of public footpaths that you followed at the start of this walk. Follow these down through fields to the road to the north of Crickhowell. Turn right and walk down the road to the Great Oak. Then turn right onto the little lane that leads you back into the centre of **Crickhowell** and the end of a long, though rewarding backpack.

25 – The Vale of Ewyas Skyline Walk

Total Distance:	38km
Daily Distances:	1) 25km 2) 13km
Maps:	OS Outdoor Leisure, sheet 13 *Brecon Beacons National Park Eastern Area*
Starting Point:	The little village of Cwmyoy at the foot of the Black Mountains (grid ref. SO 299 252), just off the A465 between Abergavenny and Hereford.

Area Summary: These are hard hills to cross, in the boggy sense. The Black Mountains have long-since had a reputation for being very wet hills indeed, and they fully deserve that accolade. You have been warned! The area is bounded to the north by the River Wye as it flows through Hay-on-Wye, to the south by the River Usk as it flows through Crickhowell, to the east by the border with England (in fact the border actually runs along the ridge of Black Mountain itself), and to the west by the Brecon Beacons.

Walk Summary: A great walk for those who love bog-trotting, although this is a much easier and shorter route

Transport:	There is no bus service to Cwmyoy
Accommodation and supplies:	There is an excellent B&B at the Queen's Head just down the valley from Cwmyoy (tel. 01873 890241), where you can also camp (grid ref. SO 311 221). Bring supplies with you or buy them in Abergavenny, Hay-on-Wye or Hereford, depending on which direction you are arriving from.
Overnight Options:	Use the Mountain Bothy Association bothy at Grwyne Fawr Reservoir, a little stone hut at the northern end (grid ref. SO 226 312).

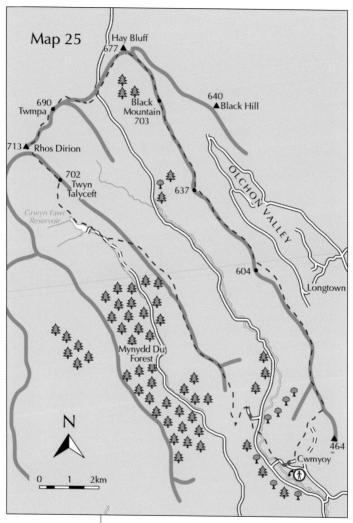

Map 25

677 Hay Bluff

690 Twmpa

713 Rhos Dirion

Black Mountain 703

640 Black Hill

702 Twyn Talyceft

637

Grwyn Fawr Reservoir

604

OLCHON VALLEY

Longtown

Mynydd Du Forest

N

0   1   2km

464

Cwmyoy

than the one taken in the previous chapter. For those who don't know the area, doing this fantastic walk first will ensure you become hooked enough to tackle the longer route in Chapter 24! The walk follows good paths and tracks for most of its length. On Day One you'll leave Cwmyoy and head for the English border on the long ridge of Black Mountain to the east. The route takes you along this ridge to Hay Bluff, overlooking the River Wye, then westwards and down to the Grwyne Fawr Reservoir where there is a bothy in which you can spend the night. On Day Two you'll leave the bothy and make for Chwarel y Fan, a low hill to the south-east. This leads onto a fine ridge that will take you all the way back to Cwmyoy.

Day One: Offa's Dyke Path to the Summit of Black Mountain

From the centre of **Cwmyoy** take the dead-end lane up towards the church on the hill, then bend round to Penywern farm on the right. From the eastern-most corner of the building a public byway climbs up the hill and passes to the right of a rocky little ridge. The route makes its way towards Ty-hwnt-y-bwlch, and then contours around the western flanks of Cwm Lau to a junction of paths and track at the head of the cwm above Blaenyoy. Here take the public footpath on the left, climbing up the steep headwall of the cwm to emerge on the flanks of Hatterrall Hill. The path bends around to the north and crosses the open moorland to join the busy Offa's Dyke Path which runs along the ridge.

The Offa's Dyke long-distance national trail closely follows a series of earthworks from Sedbury Cliffs near the Severn Bridge in the south to Prestatyn on the north coast. The earthworks were built by Offa, who was King of Mercia from 757 until his death in 796, Mercia being that huge Anglian kingdom which in the 6th century stretched from Wessex to Northumbria with Wales on its western border.

Turn northwards along Offa's Dyke and follow it down to a high col on a narrowing of the heathery ridge. The route continues northwards along the ridge, climbing again to an OS trig pillar at 552m atop a little knoll. Stick to the ridge throughout.

To the east of the ridge you look into England, and to the west into Wales. The ridge itself marks the border, and you can actually walk with one foot in each, although you'd never know it at the time as the border is unmarked other than by the eroded path on Offa's Dyke.

The ridge continues snake-like, bending and curving as it takes you in a general northwards direction. You climb gently to a spot height at 605m above Black Darren, and then continue to another OS trig pillar at 610m. Ahead the ridge swells to 616m high, and then leads you on down to a col at a pile of stones.

Contrary to initial impressions, these wild moorlands have a huge variety of interesting wildflowers growing in the peaty soil. You should look out for bilberry, cowberry, cloudberry, crowberry and tormentil, as well as ling, bell and cross-leaved heathers. The wetter parts of the moorland holds round and oval-leaved sundews, as well as butterwort, lousewort and milkwort, while any pools will usually hold clusters of bog bean.

This is a great viewpoint on a fine day. The panorama takes in the whole of the Wye Valley around Hay-on-Wye at your feet, and the distant hills of the Radnor Forest and the Cwmdeuddwr hills beyond Newbridge-on-Wye.

Now the real ascent of **Black Mountain** starts, and the route takes you up the easy south-east ridge of the mountain itself. The summit is not at all obvious, being just one of a number of peaty bumps on a fairly broad plateau. The route passes over it anyway, and then takes you down to a boggy col at Llech y Lladron.

Continue along the Offa's Dyke path from Llech y Lladron up to the fine summit of **Hay Bluff** at 677m. ◄

Keep a look out for hunting merlin as you walk along these moorland fringes. These tiny birds of prey hunt by flying very low to the ground and coming up on small birds and insects unawares. Meadow pipits and wheatears live on these moors in summer, and red grouse nest in the heather. Some common wading birds might also be there, including golden plover and lapwing.

Turn to the south-west from Hay Bluff's OS trig pillar and walk along the ridge of Ffynnon y Parc down to a road at the Gospel Pass. Bear left across the road to a track climbing up an eroded gully. Follow this out onto grass slopes above, then skirt around the edge of the escarpment to your right to the summit of Lord Hereford's Knob or **Twmpa** at 690m.

From the top of Twmpa, which is marked by a big ancient cairn, a ridge runs off to the south-west to a boggy col. Descend this ridge, then continue up the vague path beyond to the broad summit of **Rhos Dirion** at 713m.

From Rhos Dirion a very vague ridge runs away to the south-east, and you should take a compass bearing to a group of boundary stones marked on the map near to the obscure little summit of Twyn Talycefn. Follow this then continue to the summit of **Twyn Talycefn** at 702m. Here the ridge becomes more obvious, though you should head off this on a diagonally descending

Black Mountain pony

course to the head of the Grwyne Fawr Reservoir where you will find the small bothy in which you can make yourself comfortable for the night.

Day Two: The Blacksmith's Stone and Chwarel y Fan

A public byway runs along the north side of the Grwyne Fawr Reservoir and you should start the day by following this south-eastwards to the dam. From here rough, open slopes lead eastwards to the ridge between Rhos Dirion and Chwarel y Fan. There is a vague path along the ridge and you should turn right along this to a cluster of cairns at the Blacksmith's Stone. The ridge above is more obvious and the path along it soon leads you to the summit of Chwarel y Fan at a small cairn. ◄

The summit lies on top of a fine little ridge at 679m high. The name Chwarel y Fan translates as 'quarry beacon'.

The ridge continues to the south-east down to Bwlch Bach, then narrows as you walk on to Bwlch Isaf. Beyond the bwlch a little knoll rises out of the moorland. This is the little summit of Bâl-Mawr at 607m. The top has an OS trip pillar at the highest point. Drop down to the south-east to a col at Bal-Bach, then continue along the ridge to a public footpath that leads you onwards to the ancient cairn on Garn-Wen. Follow the ridge down to the south to the edge of a forest at Coed Tŷ Canol. Here there is a junction of public footpaths and you should bear left and follow the one outside the forest along the top edge of the trees. Follow this north-eastwards and down to the farm at Noyaddllwyd. At the corner of the forest by the farm buildings a public byway follows a track downhill to the south and out to the road at Ty-ddraenen. Turn left along the road for 50m to a bend left. On the right at this point there is a public byway that crosses the Afon Honddu via a bridge. Cross this and bear right at a junction onto a public footpath. This initially follows the true left bank of the stream, then follows field boundaries to the south-east to bring you out at a narrow lane at a bridge just to the west of Cwmyoy. Turn left along the lane and follow it into the village of **Cwmyoy** and the end of a great Black Mountain backpack.

BIBLIOGRAPHY

The following are recommended reading for those contemplating walking in Wales.

The High Summits of Wales, Graham Uney (Logaston Press).

The Mountains of England and Wales, Volume 1, Wales, John and Anne Nuttall (Cicerone Press).

Hillwalking in Wales (2 Volumes), Peter Hermon (Cicerone Press).

Hillwalking in Snowdonia, Steve Ashton (Cicerone Press).

Ridges of Snowdonia, Steve Ashton (Cicerone Press).

Scrambles in Snowdonia, Steve Ashton (Cicerone Press).

Map and Compass, Pete Hawkins (Cicerone Press).

The Hillwalker's Guide to Mountaineering, Terry Adby and Stuart Johnston (Cicerone Press)

USEFUL ADDRESSES

Mountain Bothy Association
General Secretary
Lynda Woods
28 Duke Street
Clackmannan
Scotland
FK10 4EF

The Welsh Tourist Board
Brunel House
2 Fitz Allan House
Cardiff
CF2 1UY

The author of this book is the Chairman of the Welsh Hewitts Club, a hillwalking club devoted to exploring the mountains, valleys and moors of Wales and elsewhere. He also runs hillwalking and wildlife holidays as well as National Navigation Award Scheme Courses for walkers. He can be contacted at:

Graham Uney
East Anglia Navigation School
Website: www.eastanglianavigation.co.uk
Email: eans@btinternet.com

SUMMARY OF WALKS

No	Walk Name	Start/ Finish Points	Total Distance	Number of Days	OS Maps	Difficulty /Grade
1	The High Carneddau	Aber Falls	42km	2	Explorer 17	3
2	The Glyderau and Southern Carneddau	Capel Curig	43km	2	Explorer 17	3
3	The Snowdon Massif	Llanberis	32km	2	Explorer 17	3
4	The Moelwynion from Dolwyddelan	Dolwyddelan	43km	2	Explorer 17 & 18	2
5	The Moel Hebog Hills and Nantlle Ridges	Cwm Pennant	31km	2	Explorer 17	2
6	The Clwydian Range from Ruthin	Ruthin	47km	2	Explorer 256	1
7	The Rhinog Traverse	Llechfraith	36km	2	Explorer 18	3
8	The Mountains of Arenig from Llyn Tegid	Llyn Tegid	77km	3	Landranger 124 & 125	3
9	The Main Ridge of the Arans	Llanuwchllyn	42km	2	Landranger 124	2
10	Around the Source of the River Dovey	Start: Llanuwchllyn Finish: Dolgellau	46km	2	Landranger 124	3
11	Cadair Idris and the Tarrens	Llanllwyda	52km	2	Landranger 124 & 135	2
12	Exploring the Ridges around the Tanat Valley	Llanrhaeadr-ym-Mochnant	53km	2	Landranger 125	2
13	The Heights of the Berwyn Range	Llanrhaeadr-ym-Mochnant	55km	2	Landranger 125	2
14	The Plynlimon Range from Staylittle	Staylittle	68km	3	Landranger 135	3
15	Pen y Garn and Cwmystwyth	Crosswodd	48km	2	Landranger 135	1

No	Walk Name	Start/ Finish Points	Total Distance	Number of Days	OS Maps	Difficulty /Grade
16	The Elan Valley Reservoirs	Elan Village TIC	43km	2	Explorer 200	2
17	The Cwmdeuddwr Hills	Rhayader	38km	2	Explorer 200	2
18	To the Source of the Afon Tywi	Ty-Mawr	44km	2	Explorer 200	2
19	Glascwm and the Radnor Forest	Glascwm	48km	2	Landranger 148	1
20	The Beacons' Northern Escarpment Traverse	Start: Brecon Finish: Sennibridge	45km	2	Explorer 12	3
21	The Mynydd Du and the Afon Twrch	Glyntawe	37km	2	Explorer 12	2
22	The Fforest Fawr from Ystradfellte	Ystradfellte	39km	2	Explorer 12	2
23	The Brecon Beacons	Pontsticill	40km	2	Explorer 12 & 13	2
24	The Black Mountains from Crickhowell	Crickhowell	48km	2	Explorer 13	3
25	The Vale of Ewyas Skyline Walk	Cwmyoy	38km	2	Explorer 13	1

NOTE The grade given for difficulty takes into account such things as length of the route, amount of height gain, navigational skills needed, presence of escape routes, and so on.

Grade 1 = Easy route suitable for all
Grade 2 = Mountain or longer route for the more adventurous
Grade 3 = Hard route only for those with backpacking and mountain experience